THE
FOUR GOSPELS
AS ONE

an interweaving of the gospels according to
SS Matthew, Mark, Luke and John

EGON PUBLISHERS LTD.

This edition published in 1996
by Egon Publishers Ltd.
Royston Road, Baldock, Herts SG7 6NW

Copyright © Egon Publishers Ltd and Wendy Marie Hearn

ISBN 0 905858 93 X

Designed and printed in England by
Streets Printers
Royston Road, Baldock, Herts SG7 6NW

NOTES SUPPLEMENTARY TO *THE FOUR GOSPELS AS ONE*

THE FOUR GOSPELS AS ONE

"This is an unusual interweaving of the Gospels. It is my hope that those who read it will become more aware of the astonishing impact of Jesus on his contemporaries and what he has to offer today".

The Most Revd and Rt Hon Dr George Carey, Archbishop of Canterbury.

"The good news of the Gospel is for telling. Any attempt to tell it more understandably and coherently is welcome. Wendy Hearn has put together the four Gospels in the continuing narrative that communicates the Gospel story compellingly.
"Seeing the events through the eyes of the four separate witnesses is invaluable. But this approach will make the story accessible to many who might not otherwise hear it. It can be an invaluable tool in sharing the facts of the Gospel record in an engaging manner."

General Paul A. Rader, The Salvation Army

"I am sure that this kind of realignment of the various Gospel presentations, in continuous-reading-form, could help many people to a first encounter with Christ through the words of Scripture".

The Rt Revd Michael Marshall, Adviser in Evangelism to the Archbishops of Canterbury and York.

"I believe this book will be invaluable as an introduction to the Gospels for young people and for those studying them for the first time. But mature Christians, even preachers and teachers, will find it a most useful tool I only wish I had had such a book to put into the hands of the people I was ministering to".

Colonel William Clark, The Salvation Army.

"I would have no hesitation in recommending this book to teachers for pupils at 'A' level and above who are making an in-depth study of the Gospels. The text is accurately portrayed, the source of the different elements is clearly indicated; and the appendices are informative".

Mrs Heather Bentley, Head of Religious Studies, Thomas Mills High School, Framlingham, Suffolk and Member of the Methodist Church.

"What a treasure it will be for the inquisitive mind. I think every household should have one and it could really be part of the curriculum for school studies. Well done, and I wish you every success – I know that charities will benefit from its sale".

Frederick Dent Esq., J.P., Grays, Essex.

"I found it a unique and very moving experience to be able to sit down and read the four Gospels as one might read any other book. The glossary is an excellent aid to the ordinary reader and gives a clear understanding of the background one needs to know".

The Revd Ben Angell, Retired Minister of the Halesworth United Reformed Church

"An inspiration to encounter comment on Scripture which proclaims 'This is Truth' and yet raises useful questions for further critical study".

Miss Cynthia Wake, M.A., Director of Education, Norwich Diocesan Board of Education

INTRODUCTION

J 3:16 *"God so loved the world that he gave his only Son, so that all who believe in him may not die, but have ever lasting life."*

Thousands of books have been written about the Bible, but the basis of all Christian belief is to be found in the gospels written by SS Matthew, Mark, Luke and John. These are our only reliable source of information about Jesus Christ, the Son of God. The more we study these gospels, and the more we learn about Jesus and his teaching, the better we are able to use this knowledge to assess the truth and importance of everything else. Without this knowledge we are at a loss.

The Four Gospels As One is not "another book about the Bible" or "story of the gospels"; it is an interweaving of the gospels themselves, and is designed to be an introduction to them for people who are studying them for the first time – especially for those who do not take readily to study or reading. It is not intended to replace the gospels, but should be used as a working manual, and to refer its readers to the versions which they already have.

Many people know the gospels so well that, when they are reading one of them, they remember the variations and additions, which exist in the other three, and all four versions weave themselves together in their minds like a great fugue. And some have no need of any modern translation because the truth has already come to them through the King James Bible (the Authorised Version), and they often cling to the 'Old' English for this very good reason. These people, too, may find refreshment in reading the combined accounts of all four gospels as one.

The gospels differ, in detail as well as in chronology, as independent accounts of events given by different witnesses nearly always do – even today, when we can use cameras to record events. But we know that the gospel writers all loved the central figure in their story, and that He is Truth; and patient study reveals that these differing accounts complement rather than contradict each other.

The texts are arranged, as far as possible, in chronological order and in modern English; and full reference to the gospels will be found in the margin of the main text, the Reference Tables and the People Index.

Supplementary Notes, maps and plans provide a small amount of historical and geographical background. It would be helpful to look at these notes before starting on the Gospel, especially at those marked # in the index. The others contain items of relevant historical interest, with special reference to places of worship.

If we follow the commands of Jesus we will continue to commend the Gospel to all people everywhere. It speaks of the Way, the Truth and the Life; and it is the most important news in the world because it concerns the immortal soul of each one of us.

J 1:9   *"The Light shines for every man."*

1996   WENDY MARIE HEARN
                                             Compiler

For the children:

THE FOUR GOSPELS

The four gospels are like a treasure chest full of jewels. Reading through *The Four Gospels As One* may help you to see and understand them better.

You will then need to examine the 'jewels' more closely; and as you study them one by one, their glowing colours will light up for you. Some are like strings of pearls, while others sparkle and make you want to laugh; and others of them are so heavy that it hurts even to hold them. But even the heaviest are surrounded with such beauty that the whole treasure chest shines with a powerful glory.

G
(comfort)

This power, if you seek it with all your heart, will guide and comfort you through dark and difficult times and places, as well as the happy ones, all through your life, and may even help the people around you, too.

Many parts of the Gospel are like stories. You know that some stories are only pretend – but these are true. Mingled with the stories are snatches of conversation, and things that happened in Jesus' life here on this planet, Earth. These were remembered and treasured by his friends, and often used when they were spreading the Good News about the Kingdom of Heaven and how Jesus came to show us the way there.

It is thanks to these men, women and children, and to the work of the Holy Spirit through those who have followed the Way all down the centuries, that we are able to read them today and to find our way to the greatest Treasure of all.

G =

You will find this word in the Glossary (page ii in the Supplementary Notes at the end of this book).

In the margins of the main text you will find other references which tell you where in the Bible you can find the text you are reading.

p. xx
para 3

M = Matthew; Mk = Mark; L = Luke; J = John. In the Supplementary Notes J stands for Josephus.

The symbols « » are used instead of inverted commas for words spoken by God. Words in brackets ( ) are extra to the text.

SOURCES

Main Text

The King James Bible (the Authorised Version)
The New English Bible – the Revised English Bible
The Moffatt Translation of the Bible – Dr James Moffatt
The Good News Bible

Supplementary Notes

A Complete Concordance of the Old and New Testament
– Alexander Cruden 1737
The Apocrypha
The Oxford Bible Atlas
Jesus and His Times – Reader's Digest
Illustrated Bible Dictionary

Many thanks also to

The Very Revd H. A. R. Edgell, O.St.J., A.K.C.
(Prior to the Abbey of St Benet-at-Holme, Norfolk)
Barbara Nunns, B.Ed. Hons.(Lond)
Vera Frampton
Pamela Swinyard
Mavis McDougall
R. F. Lawrence
S.F. Youngs

CONTENTS

THE FOUR GOSPELS AS ONE   pages 1-120
Appendix

Reference Tables
People Index

Supplementary Notes   pages (i) – (xxxviii)

Please look at these notes and maps before starting on
the main text, especially at those marked # in the index.
The others contain snippets of relevant historical interest,
with special reference to places of worship.

The Gospel of Jesus Christ,
The Son of God,
according to
Matthew, Mark, Luke and John

Before the world was made the Word was there. He was with God, and he was part of God. And everything was made by him. Not one thing that exists was made without him.

The Word held Life; and everything that lives came to be alive with His Life. And that Life is the Light of mankind.

The Light shines in the darkness, and yet the darkness does not know it. But the darkness can never diminish it.

There appeared a man named John, sent from God. He came as a witness to testify to the Light, that all might become believers through him. He was not the Light. The real Light, which shines for every man, was even then coming into the world.

He was in the world, but the world, though it owed its being to him, did not know him.

But all who did receive him, and those who knew who he was and believed in him – to them he gave the right to become children of God – born, not of blood, nor of the will of the flesh, nor of the will of man – but of God.

So the Word became flesh. He came to dwell among us; and we saw his glory – glory such as befits the Father's only Son, full of grace and truth. Out of his full store we have all received grace upon grace; for while the Law was given through Moses, grace and truth came through Jesus Christ.

No one has ever seen God but God's only Son. He who is nearest to the Father's heart, he has made him known.

In the days of Herod, King of Judea, there lived an old priest called Zechariah. He was one of the Abijah order of the priesthood. His wife, Elizabeth, came from another priestly family; she was one of the daughters of Aaron. And they lived in one of the small hill towns of Judea.

They were good, upright people, who devoutly followed the Lord's commandments and strictly observed all the laws of Jewish Temple ritual. Both were getting on in years, and they had come to accept, with great sadness, that all their hopes of having children had been in vain. Elizabeth was barren.

See plan
page xxix
L 1:8 One day when, in accordance with priestly custom, Zechariah's division was on duty in the Temple, it was his privilege to offer incense in the Sanctuary. Everything was as usual; all the people in the congregation were at prayer in the outer part of the Temple at the time of incense. When Zechariah entered the Sanctuary to approach the altar of incense – there – standing to the right of the altar – was an angel of the Lord.

Zechariah was much shaken and very frightened; but the angel said, "Don't be afraid, Zechariah. Your prayer has been heard; your wife will bear you a son, and your heart will be full of joy. Indeed, many will be glad that he was born, for he will be great in God's eyes. You must call him 'John'; and he must never touch wine or strong drink. From his birth he will be filled with the Holy Spirit, and he will bring back many of the people of Israel to the Lord their God. He will be God's herald, possessed by the spirit and Mal 4:6 power of Elijah, to reconcile fathers with their children, to turn back God's disobedient children into the ways of righteousness, and to prepare the people so that they may be ready and fit for the Lord."

"But – how I can believe this?" said Zechariah. "I am an old man . . . . my wife is getting on in years . . ."

The angel replied, "I am Gabriel. I stand in the very presence of God. And I have been sent to bring you these glad tidings. And behold! Because you have not believed my words you will be deprived of the power of speech – until the day when those words will come true – whether you believe it or not."

All this time the people in the Temple were waiting for Zechariah to reappear; and they could not think what was keeping him so long. He finally emerged from the Sanctuary, dazed, and unable to speak; and they realised that he had had a vision.

When his spell of Temple duty was over Zechariah went home. Soon afterwards Elizabeth conceived; and for five months she lived in seclusion. "This is God's work," she thought. "At last he has spared me this reproach among men."

L 1:26 Six months later God sent his angel, Gabriel, to Nazareth, a town in Galilee. This time the message he carried was to a young girl who was betrothed to a man called Joseph, a descendant of King David. The angel went to Mary's house and greeted her. "Peace be with you, Mary," he said. "Most favoured of women, the Lord is with you." Mary was alarmed by these words, and bewildered. "Don't be frightened, Mary," the angel said. "You have found favour with God. You are to conceive and bear a Son; and you are to call him – Jesus. He will be called the Son of the Most High. The Lord will give him the throne of David, and he will be King of Israel for ever. His reign will have no end."

Mary said, "But I am a virgin. How can this be?" Gabriel answered, "The Holy Spirit will come upon you, and the power of the Most High will overshadow you. And this holy child you are to bear will therefore be called the son of God.

"Remember your cousin, Elizabeth – she who was thought to be barren has conceived a son in her old age, and is now already in her sixth month. With God, nothing is impossible."

Mary replied, "I am the Lord's servant. As you have spoken, so be it." And the angel departed.

Mary wasted no time. She went straight away to Zechariah's house in the hills to see Elizabeth. When Elizabeth heard Mary's happy words of greeting, the baby in her womb stirred; and she was filled with the Holy Spirit, and cried out in a loud voice:

"Blessed are you among women! Blessed is the child you will bear! Who am I that the mother of my Lord should come to visit me? I tell you, when your greeting sounded in my ears the babe in my womb leapt for joy. Blessed is she who believed that the Lord's words would be fulfilled!"

And Mary said, "My heart sings with praise to the Lord, and my spirit is full of joy in God, my Saviour; so tenderly has he looked upon his servant, humble though she is. From this day forth all peoples will call me blessed, so wonderfully has he dealt with me; and holy is his name. His mercy is upon generation after generation to all who honour him. He has showed the strength of his arm, and has scattered the proud in the conceit of their scheming hearts. He has put down mighty rulers, and he has honoured the humble and meek. He has filled the hungry with good things, and the rich he has sent empty away. He has come to the help of his servant, Israel, remembering his promise to our forefathers – to show mercy to Abraham, and his children's children for ever!"

Mary stayed with Elizabeth for about three months, and then she returned home to Nazareth.

L 1:57   The time came for Elizabeth's child to be born, and she gave birth to a son. When her family and friends heard how the Lord had shown this great favour to her they all rejoiced with her; and on the eighth day they came to circumcise the child. They were about to name him Zechariah, after his father; but his mother said,

"No. He is to be called John." "But there's no one in your family called John," they said. They turned to Zechariah and asked him what he wanted the baby's name to be. He asked for a writing tablet, and then, to everyone's amazement, he wrote: "His name is John". At that instant his voice was returned to him, and he began to speak, praising God. His family and friends stood, awestruck. Soon everyone in the uplands of Judea was talking about it; and all who heard it were deeply moved, and wondered what the child was destined to become – for clearly the hand of the Lord was upon him . . .

L 1:67 Zechariah was filled with the Holy Spirit, and prophesied (concerning Jesus): "Blessed be the Lord God of Israel! For he has come to his people; and he has saved them and set them free; and has raised up a deliverer of mighty power from the house of his servant, David – as he promised, through the mouths of his holy prophets, age after age from ancient times, that he would deliver us from our enemies, and from the power of those who hate us; that he would show mercy to our forefathers, and remember his sacred covenant. Such was the solemn promise he made to our father, Abraham, that he would rescue us from the hands of our enemies; and that he would allow us to serve him, free from fear, and to worship him in holiness and uprightness of heart, all our days.

"And you, my child, you shall be called the prophet of the Highest; for you will be the Lord's forerunner, to prepare his way, and lead his people to salvation through knowledge of him, by the

G forgiveness of their ⸰sins. Thanks to the tender compassion of our God, who will cause the dayspring from heaven to visit us, to shine on those who sit in darkness, and in the shadow of death, and to guide our feet into the way of peace."

L 1:80 And the child grew, and he became strong in the Spirit; and he
G lived in the desert¹ until the time when he appeared in public to the people of Israel.

M 1:18 The birth of Jesus Christ came about in this way: his mother, Mary, was betrothed to Joseph. Before their marriage she found that she was with child by the Holy Spirit. Joseph was a man of principle, but at the same time he had no wish to expose Mary to public disgrace; so he resolved to have the marriage contract set aside quietly. But, after he had formed this decision, the angel of the Lord appeared to him in a dream; and the angel said to him, "Joseph, son of David, do not be afraid to take Mary to be your wife; for it is by the Holy Spirit that she has conceived. She will bear a Son, and you shall call him Jesus – for he will save his people from their sins."

Isa. 7:14
All this happened in exact fulfilment of the word of the Lord, spoken through his prophet Isaiah: "« A virgin shall conceive and bear a Son, and shall call his name Emmanuel – God is with us»"

G «»

Joseph, waking from sleep, did as the angel had said. He took Mary home to be his wife, but the marriage was not consummated until after her Son was born. And he named the child Jesus.

•see p.(v)
In those days a decree was issued by the Emperor Augustus* that a census should be taken of all the people in the Roman world . . .

L 2:1
This all took place when Quirinius was Governor of Syria, and it was the first registration of its kind. Everyone had to be registered in his own home town; so Joseph and Mary had to travel from

map p. (xvii) Nazareth in Galilee to Bethlehem, the City of David, because Joseph was of the House of David.

When they reached Bethlehem, the time had come for Mary's baby to be born. There was no room at the inn, and Mary gave birth to her first-born Son in a stable. She wrapped him in swathing bands, and laid him in a manger.

G

In the fields around Bethlehem that night there were shepherds keeping watch over their flocks – when, suddenly, the angel of the Lord stood before them, and the glory of the Lord was shining all around them. They were terror-stricken. But the angel said to them, "Don't be afraid! For I have brought glad tidings – of great joy to all the people of the world. For, this very night, in the City of David, your Saviour is born – Christ, the Lord! And, so that you may know how to find him, you will find the baby, wrapped in his swaddling bands, lying in a manger."

And, suddenly there was with the angel, a myriad of the heavenly host, singing praises to God – "Glory to God in Highest Heaven! On earth – peace! Good will to all men upon whom his favour rests!"

When the angel had departed from them, the shepherds said to each other, "Let's go and find him! Let's go to Bethlehem – now, and see for ourselves this wonderful thing that the Lord has told us." They ran into the town and found their way to Joseph and Mary, and – just as the angel had said – the baby was lying in a manger. And they remembered what the angel had told them about this child . . . "A Saviour – who is Christ, the Lord!" They told everyone of what they had seen and heard, and all who heard it were filled with awe. Then they returned to their flocks, praising God.

L 2:21   A week later the time came for the baby to be circumcised; and he was named – Jesus – the name announced by the angel before his conception.

And, after the period of purification had been completed (according to Mosaic Law), Mary and Joseph took the baby to Jerusalem to 'present him to the Lord' – as it is written in God's Law: 'Every first-born male child shall be consecrated to the Lord.' The Law also required an offering to be made – either a pair of turtle doves or two young pigeons.

In Jerusalem there lived a man called Simeon. He loved God, and he was a good man. He had watched and hoped and waited all his life for Israel to be restored to her own people. He had been told by the Holy Spirit that he would see the Lord's Messiah before he died. The Holy Spirit made sure that Simeon was in the Temple when Mary and Joseph brought Jesus, in obedience to the Law. He took the baby in his arms and gave thanks to God: "Lord, now let your servant depart in peace as you promised. For I have seen your salvation with my own eyes – the Deliverance you have prepared for all the world – to be a light of revelation to the Gentiles, and to be the glory of your people Israel."

Mary and Joseph were very much surprised by these unexpected words from Simeon. The old man blessed them. Then he said to Mary, "This child is destined to bring about the downfall of many people in Israel, and also to bring salvation to many. He will be a sign – which many will reject. And you, too, Mary will be pierced to the heart by sorrow. And the secret thoughts of many will be laid bare."

G

At that moment an aged lady came into the Temple. This was Anna, the prophetess, daughter of Phanuel of the tribe of Asher. She was now very old, having been married for seven years and widowed for eighty-four. In all those years she had never left the Temple, but had worshiped God day and night, fasting and praying. She also gave thanks to God; and thenceforth she told all who were awaiting the liberation of Jerusalem about the infant Jesus.

L 2:39   When they had finished their observance of all the rites required by the Law of God, they went home.

M 2:1   Soon after Jesus was born, some wise men from the east arrived in Jerusalem. They were astrologers, and they were asking everyone where they could find the baby who was born to be King of the Jews. "We saw his star when it rose in the east," they said, "and we have come to pay homage to him."

This caused much agitation among the citizens of Jerusalem; and when it came to the ears of King Herod, he found it the most disquieting news he had heard for a long time. It made him very nervous. He sent for the chief priests and experts in Jewish Law and asked them, "Where will the Messiah be born?" "In Bethlehem," they replied . . ." The scriptural reference is as follows: the prophet writes: « And thou, Bethlehem, in the land of Judah, art not least among the princes of Judah, for out of thee shall come a Governor that shall rule my people Israel! »"

Micah 5:2

Herod called the astrologers from the east to a private meeting and questioned them about the appearance of the star, and when it had first been seen. Then he sent them on their way to Bethlehem saying, "Go and make a careful search for the child; and when you find him, you must come and let me know so that I, too, may go and pay homage to him."

The wise men listened to the King and then went on their way. And the star went ahead of them until it hung over the place where the child lay. When they saw the star they were filled with joy. They went into the house and found the child with Mary, his mother; and they knelt down and worshipped him. Then they opened their treasures and offered him gifts – gold, frankincense and myrrh. But, as they slept that night, they were warned, in a dream, not to return to Herod. They went home by a different route.

After they had left, the angel of the Lord appeared to Joseph in a dream. "Get up, Joseph!" he was saying. "You must take Mary and the baby into Egypt; and be prepared to stay there until I come to you again, for Herod will be searching for the child, to kill him." Joseph got up at once and, by daybreak, the Holy Family were well on their way into Egypt, where they remained until the death of Herod. And so it was that the prophecy came to be fulfilled: « Out of Egypt have I called my Son. »

Hosea 11:1

After waiting in vain for the return of the wise men, it dawned upon Herod that he had been tricked and he was furious. In a towering passion he gave orders that all the children under two years old, in and around Bethlehem, were to be killed. This was in accordance with the date of the star's first appearance as given by the wise men. (Legend has it that Mary wept over this 'massacre of the innocents' and the anguish of their parents). The tragic words

Jer. 31:15

of Jeremiah were fulfilled: "« In Rama was there a voice heard; lamentation and great weeping – Rachel weeping for her children, and refusing all consolation, because – they are not . . . »"

When Herod died, the angel came again to Joseph. "Arise now, Joseph, and take the child and his mother and return to the land of Israel; for the men who threatened the child's life are now dead." So Joseph arose and brought them back to the land of Israel; but he felt uneasy about returning to Bethlehem because he knew that Herod's son, Archelaus, had succeeded his father as ruler of Judea. And, being warned, again in a dream, he went on to Galilee and settled in Nazareth. And thus they came to fulfil another prophecy:

M 2:23

"He shall be called a Nazarene."

L 2:40

And the child grew and became strong. His spirit was full of wisdom, and the grace of God was upon him.

L 2:41

Every year Jesus' parents travelled with family and friends to Jerusalem for the Passover Festival; and when he was twelve, they made the pilgrimage as usual. After the Festival was over they started for home; but, though his parents did not know it, Jesus was still in Jerusalem. Thinking that he was with others in the family, they travelled for a whole day before they began to worry about not having seen him. Unable to find him among their relatives and friends, they returned to Jerusalem to look for him.

The search took three days. They finally found him, to their astonishment, seated in the Temple, surrounded by Jewish teachers. He was listening to them and putting questions to them. And all who heard him were amazed at his knowledge, and the intelligence of his answers to their questions.

Mary said to Jesus, "My son, how could you do this to us? Your father and I have been very worried – we have been searching for you everywhere." Jesus said to her, "But – where ever were you looking for me? Didn't you realise that I was bound to be in my Father's house?" But they did not fully understand what he was saying to them.

They all went back to Nazareth, and Jesus grew up under his parents' authority. But his mother treasured up all these things in her heart, and often wondered about them.

And Jesus grew in wisdom and in stature, and in favour with God and man.

M 3:4
Mk 1:6
L 1:15

The archangel, Gabriel, had told Zechariah before his son was born that from his birth the boy would be filled with the Holy Spirit and, also, that he was to drink no wine or strong drink. John

L 1:80   lived in the desert from an early age. He wore a rough coat of camel's hair, and a leather belt round his waist; and he ate locusts and wild honey.

L 3:1   When the word of God came to John in the desert, Tiberius was

map p. xvii in his fifteenth year as Emperor; Pontius Pilate was Governor of Judea; Herod Antipas was Tetrarch of Galilee and his brother,

G   Philip, was Tetrarch□ of Iturea and Trachonitis; Lysanias was Tetrarch of Abilene. Annas and Caiaphas were High Priests.

L 1:15   In those days, inspired by the Holy Spirit, and by Elijah, John

and 17 G began to preach in the wilderness□ of Judea, calling upon the

M 3:1   people to turn away from their sins. "Repent!" he said. "For the

Mk 1:4   kingdom of Heaven is very close to you. Be baptised as a token of

L 3:3   your repentance, and God will forgive your sins." And the people

L 3:18   flocked to him from the Jordan valley and the city of Jerusalem, and from all of Judea, confessing their sins; and he baptised them in the River Jordan.

      He gave scant courtesy to these people, especially to the many

L 3:7 G □Pharisees and □Sadduces he saw coming for baptism. "You generation of vipers!" he said. "Who told you that you could escape the wrath to come?" And he said, "Then prove that your repentance is real – let's see some of the fruits of this repentance! And don't start saying to yourselves, 'We are the Sons of Abraham.' I tell you – God can make children for Abraham out of these stones here!

      "The trees are being felled – the axe is already laid to their roots – and any tree that bears poor fruit gets cut down and thrown on the fire."

      The people asked him, "Then what are we to do?"

L 3:10   John replied, "Whoever has two shirts must share with the man who has none. And anyone who has food must do the same."

      There were tax-collectors among them, and they said to him, "Master, what should we do?" "Take only the fair amount of tax due from the people, no more," he said. Soldiers asked him, "What about us?" And he said to them, "No bullying. No blackmail – and – be content with your pay."

L 3:15   People's hopes began to rise. They were wondering about John – whether perhaps he could be the Messiah they had all longed for. But John said to them, "I baptise you with water; but after me will come One who is mightier than I am. I'm not worthy even to tie his shoes."

M 3:13   Jesus went to the Jordan from Galilee and came to John to

Mk 1:9   be baptised by him. John tried to stop him. "You come to me?" he

9

L 3:21   said. "I need to be baptised by you." But Jesus replied, "Let it be so for the present. It is right that we should fulfil all that God requires of us." And John baptised Jesus.

When Jesus came up out of the water after his baptism, he was praying; and, at that moment, the heavens opened and the Spirit of God descended, like a dove, to alight upon him; and a voice came from heaven saying « This is my son, my Beloved, upon whom my favour rests. »

M 4:1   Then Jesus returned from the Jordan and was led by the Spirit
Mk 1:12   into the wilderness where he remained, among the wild animals,
L 4:1 G   for forty days; and all the time the ▢devil was there – tempting him. And when the forty days were ended, having had nothing to eat, he realised that he was famished.The devil was at his side at once. "Hungry, are you? Well, if you're the Son of God you have only to order these stones here to turn into bread . . ." Jesus answered him with words from the Scriptures: " 'Man doth not live by bread
Deut 8:3   alone, but by every word that proceedeth out of the mouth of the Lord doth man live'."

Then the devil took him to the Holy City of Jerusalem and set
G   him upon the highest pinnacle▢ of the Temple. "Now," he said, "if you are God's Son – you can prove it: you can throw yourself down
Psa. 91:11   from here. The Scripture says, 'For he shall give his angels charge over thee to keep thee in all thy ways. They shall bear thee up in
Deut. 6:16   their hands, lest thou dash thy foot against a stone'." Jesus
•tempt=put   answered, "But the scripture says: 'Ye shall not tempt* the Lord
to the test   your God'."

The devil then took him to a very high mountain where he could see all the kingdoms of the world in all their splendour. "All this can be yours," he said. "It is in my power to arrange it. All you have to do is – kneel and worship me . . ." Then Jesus answered, "It is
Deut. 10:20   written: 'Thou shalt worship the Lord your God, and him only shalt thou serve'."

So, having come to the end of his temptation, the devil left him – biding his time.

And angels came and ministered to Jesus.

J 1:19   When the chief priests heard that John was calling the Jews to repentance, and that he was baptising them in Bethany (Bethabara – on the east bank of the River Jordan), they sent a deputation of priests and Levites to investigate.

"Who are you?" they asked, "I'm not the Messiah," John replied. "Who are you, then? Are you Elijah?" "Not, I am not,"
Deut 18:15   said John; (but the power of Elijah was with him). "Are you that

Prophet we are waiting for?" "No," he said. They conferred. "You must tell us who you are," they said. "We have to take an answer back to those who sent us. What do you call yourself?" John

Mk 1:2
M 3:3
Isa. 40:3

answered, "I'll tell you what I am: I am 'the voice of one crying in the wilderness, "Make straight the way of the Lord!" ' – those are Isaiah's words."

Some Pharisees who were in the deputation said to him, "If you are not the Messiah, or Elijah, the prophet, why are you baptising people?" "I am baptising with water," John replied. "But One is

L 3:16

among you, though you don't know him – One who is to come after me – and I am not worthy even to undo his shoes. He will baptise you with the Holy Spirit and with fire . . . His winnowing fan is in his hand to winnow the threshing floor. He will gather the wheat into his granary, but the chaff he will burn – on unquenchable fire."

All this took place at Bethany, where John was baptising.

J 1:29
(J 1:15)

The following day John the Baptist saw Jesus coming towards him. "Look!" he said to his disciples. "There is the Lamb of God. He is the one who is going to take away the sins of the world – the One I was talking about when I said, 'After me is coming a man who is greater than I am.' He existed before I was born. Even I didn't know who he would be – but the whole reason that I came, baptising with water, was that he should be revealed to Israel.

"The One who sent me – to baptise with water – said to me: « When you see the Spirit alight upon someone – and rest on him – you will know that he is the One who will baptise with the Holy Spirit. » And now – I have seen it. I tell you, he is the Son of God. I saw the Spirit come down from heaven, like a fluttering dove, and rest on him."

And again, the following day, John was standing with two of his disciples when Jesus passed by. "Look!" said John. "There is the Lamb of God."

J 1:37

G

When John's two disciples heard him say this, they followed Jesus. He turned and saw them following him. "What are you looking for?" he asked. They answered, "Rabbi, where are you staying?" Jesus said, "Come and see." So they went with him to see where he was staying and spent the rest of the day with him – it was about four o'clock.

One of the two was Andrew, Simon's brother. The first thing he did was to look for Simon, and when he had found him he said, "We have found the Messiah!" – which is the Hebrew for 'Christ.' And he brought Simon to Jesus. Jesus looked steadily at him. "You

M16:18   are Simon, son of John," he said. "Your name shall be 'Peter'."*

J 1:43   The next day Jesus decided to go into Galilee; and here he found

*Gk. Cephas Philip. He said to him, "Come with me." Philip, like Andrew and

L. Petra = Peter, came from Bethsaida.

rock; stone   Philip went to find Nathaniel (Bartholomew), and told him, "We
have found the man spoken of by Moses in the book of the Law, and
of whom the prophets spoke. He is Jesus, son of Joseph, from
Nazareth." "Nazareth!" said Nathaniel. "Can anything good come
out of Nazareth?" "Come and see," said Philip.

When Jesus saw Nathaniel coming he said to the others, "Now
there's a true Israelite! – straight as a die . . ." When Nathaniel
heard this he said, "How do you know me?" Jesus said, "Even when
Philip called to you I saw you – under the fig tree there." Nathaniel
said, "Rabbi! You are the Son of God! You are the King of Israel!"
Jesus said, "Is it because I said that I saw you under the fig tree
that you believe me? – You will see much greater things than that."
Then he added, "I tell you all, in very truth, you will see the
heavens open, and God's angels ascending and descending to the
Son of Man."

L 3:23   At this time Jesus was about thirty years old; and he was the
son, so people thought, of Joseph, who was a descendant of King
David – as follows:

See also   ADAM, Seth, Enos, Cainan, Mahalalel. Jared, Enoch,

p. xxxvi   Methuselah, Lamech, Noah, Shem, Arphaxad, Cainan, Shelah,
Eber, Peleg, Reu, Serug, Nahor, Terah, Abraham, Isaac, Jacob,
Judah, Perez, Hezron, Arni, Admin, Aminadab, Nahson, Salmon,
Boaz. Obed, Jesse, DAVID, Nathan, Mattatha, Menna, Melea,
Eliakim, Jonam, Joseph, Judah, Simeon, Levi, Matthat, Jorim,
Eliezer, Joshua, Er, Elmadam, Cosam, Addi, Melchi, Neri,
Shealtiel, Zerubbabel, Rhesa, Joannan, Joda, Josech, Semein,
Mattathias, Maath, Naggai, Esli, Nahum, Amos, Mattathias,
Joseph, Jannai, Melchi, Levi, Matthat, Heli – JOSEPH.

L 4:14   Jesus began preaching in the synagogues in Galilee. The power
of the Holy Spirit was with him, and all who heard him praised
him; and the news of his teaching spread fast throughout the
countryside.

L 5:1   One day, as Jesus stood on the shore of Lake Gennesaret
(Galilee) talking to the people, such a crowd gathered round him
that he was looking round for somewhere to stand so that they
could all see him. There were two boats pulled up on the beach; the
fishermen were busy washing their nets. So Jesus got into one of
the boats – it was Simon's – and he asked him to take the boat

a little way from the water's edge. Then he sat down in the boat and went on with his teaching from there.

When he had finished speaking to the people Jesus said, "Now, Simon, take the boat out further, into deep water, and let down your nets for a catch." Simon said, "Master, we've been fishing all night, and caught nothing – but, if you say so, we'll let the nets down again." And Simon and his brother, Andrew, and the rest of the crew took the boat out into the lake and cast the nets once more. This time, to their amazement, they caught so many fish that the net was breaking. They signalled to their partners in the other boat to come quickly and help them; and they all struggled to bring in the catch. There were so many fish that the boats were loaded to the point of sinking.

When he realised what had happened, Simon fell on his knees before Jesus and said, "Go away from me, Lord, for I am a sinful man." He and the others could hardly believe the size of this catch. Jesus said to Simon and Andrew, "Come with me – and I'll teach you to be fishers of men!" They beached the boats, and then left

M 4:18
Mk 1:16

everything and followed him. Jesus also called their partners, James and John, the sons of Zebedee; and they, too, followed Jesus, leaving their father in the boat with the hired crew.

J 2:1
G

There was a wedding in Cana, in Galilee. Mary, the mother of Jesus, was there; and Jesus and his disciples were also invited. Halfway through the reception, Mary came to her son in great anxiety. "They've run out of wine!" she said. "Don't you worry about it, Mother," he replied. "It's not my time for miracles yet." Mary went to see the servants. "Whatever he tells you to do," she said, "you do it."

Now there were six stone jars standing there, each of which had contained about twenty gallons of water. This water was used for ritual washing – ceremonies of purification required by the Jewish religious laws. Jesus said to the servants, "Fill these with water." They filled them brim-full. "Now," said Jesus, "Draw some off and take it to the master of the ceremonies." They did exactly as they were told, and the master of the ceremonies tasted it. It was wine. He did not know where this wine had come from – but the servants did. He called to the bridegroom, "What's this? We generally serve the best wine first, and when the guests have drunk a fair amount – then we bring on the ordinary stuff! But you have saved the best till last!"

And thus it was, in Cana, that the first of the signs was performed by which Jesus' disciples realised his power and glory, and came to believe in him.

J 2:12   Jesus then went to Capernaum for a few days with his mother, brothers and his disciples.

M 21:12
Mk 11:15
L 19:45
J 2:13   It was almost time for the Feast of the Passover and Jesus (with many others) went to Jerusalem. He went to the Temple and there he saw cashiers sitting at their tables and men doing a great trade selling cattle, sheep and pigeons. He poured out the coins of the money-changers and overturned their tables and the stools of the pigeon sellers. Making a small whip out of pieces of cord, he drove all the sheep and cattle out of the Temple. He said to the pigeon-sellers, "Take those out of here!" And he would not allow anyone carrying any goods to use the Temple courts as a thoroughfare. He told them all, "It is written in the Scriptures that God said « My house is to be a house of prayer for all peoples » and you have turned it into a den of thieves!" His disciples were reminded of the words in Holy Writ: 'My concern for your house, O God, burns in me like fire!'

P xxvi   Jesus taught in the Temple every day; and the Scribes came to him in great indignation. They said, "What sign of authority can you show us that gives you the right to act like this?" Jesus turned to them. "Destroy this Temple," he said, "and I will rebuild it in three days." "Oh yes?" they said. "It's taken us forty-six years to build this Temple, and you propose to rebuild it in three days?!" No one realised that the 'Temple' Jesus was talking about was his own body. It was not until after his resurrection that the disciples remembered his words and understood what they meant and their reference to the Scriptures.

Mk 11:18
L 19:47   As Jesus continued teaching in the Temple, the chief priests, the Scribes and leading citizens wanted him killed; but they could think of no way in which this could be done because he was constantly surrounded by the people, who followed him about, determined not to miss a single word.

J 2:23   During that Passover Festival many believed in him when they saw the signs that he performed; but Jesus did not trust himself to them. He knew them too well – in fact, so well that no one needed to tell him about any man – he already knew.

J 3:1   One of the Pharisees, a man called Nicodemus, a member of the Jewish Council, came to see Jesus – after dark.

Jesus said to Nicodemus, "Truly, I tell you this: a man can never see the Kingdom of God unless he is first re-born." "Rabbi," said Nicodemus, "we know that you must be a teacher sent by God because no one could perform miracles as you do unless God were with him – but – how can a man be born again when he is old? He can't get back into his mother's womb and be born again a second time!" Jesus said, "Nevertheless it is true. No one can enter the Kingdom of God unless he is born of water and Spirit. Flesh and blood can only give birth to – flesh and blood. Spirit has to give birth to Spirit. So it is not really surprising when I say to you that you must all be born again.

"Think of the wind – it blows where it likes; you can hear it, but you don't know where it has come from – or where it's going. So it is with everyone who is born of the Spirit." Nicodemus said, "I can't see how that can be . . ." "What?" said Jesus. "Do you mean to tell me that a great teacher of Israel can't understand that? These are facts I am telling you. No one has ever been to heaven except the Son of Man – that is where he came from. 'We speak of what we know, and tell you of what we have seen, but you will not accept what we say.' But if you don't believe me when I tell you about things of this world, how will you ever believe me when I'm telling you about things in heaven?

Numbers
21:9

"Just as the serpent was lifted up by Moses in the wilderness, so in the same way the Son of Man must be lifted up – so that everyone who has faith in him may not die, but have eternal life.

J3:16

For God so loved the world that he gave his only Son, so that all who believe in him may not die – but have eternal life.

"God sent his Son into the world – not to judge it – but to save it. The man who puts his trust in him is not judged; but whoever refuses to believe is judged already because he has not believed in God's only Son. The verdict follows this test. the Light has come into the world, but some men prefer darkness because their deeds are evil; and the man who does evil hates the Light – he won't come near it because it lights up his evil deeds for all to see. But

J 3:21

whoever does what is honest and true is drawn to the Light – happy in the knowledge that the Light will only show that his works were done in obedience to God's will."

After this, Jesus and his disciples went into Judea. They stayed there for some time, and people came to them to be baptised. John the Baptist also was baptising people at this time at Aenon, near Salim, where water was plentiful. People were constantly coming to him for baptism. This was before John was thrown into prison.

Some of John's disciples came to see him about a question which had arisen between themselves and the Jews about purification; and they said to John, "Rabbi, the man who was with you on the other side of the Jordan – the one you bore witness to –

(J 4:2) he is baptising now, and the crowds are flocking to him" – though actually it was the disciples who were baptising – not Jesus himself.

John said, "A man can have nothing unless it is given to him from heaven. I told you, didn't I, that I am not the Messiah? I am the one who has been sent ahead of him. It is the bridegroom to whom the bride belongs . . . the best man just stands by and listens, and is glad when he hears the bridegroom's voice. And this perfect joy is now mine. As he grows greater, so I become less important.

J 3:31 "He who comes from above is the greatest of all. A man who comes from the earth belongs to the earth and talks about earthly things. But he who comes from heaven – the One who is above all – he is telling what he has seen and heard. Some people are not believing him; but those who accept his words are simply recognising that God speaks true. For the One God sent speaks God's words – God has given him the spirit in infinite abundance. The Father loves the Son and has given him total power; and whoever puts his faith in the Son has hold of eternal life. But he who disobeys the Son will never know that life. God's wrath will remain upon him for ever."

J 4:1 Word reached the Pharisees that Jesus was winning and baptising more disciples than John. When Jesus heard what was being said, he left Judea and set out once again for Galilee; and on his way to Galilee he had to pass through Samaria. He came to a Samaritan town called Sychar, which is not far from the field which Jacob gave to his son, Joseph, with the spring called Jacob's well.

It was about midday when Jesus sat down by the well. The disciples had gone into the town to buy some food. When a Samaritan woman came to the well to draw water, Jesus asked her to give him some to drink. The woman said, "What! You, a Jew, are asking me, a Samaritan, for a drink?" – Jews and Samaritans did not mix, and would never think of sharing the same cup. Jesus said to the woman, "If you only knew what God can give, and who it is that is asking you for a drink, you would have asked him instead; and he would have given you living water." "But sir," the woman replied, "you haven't got a bucket – and this well is deep. How could you give me this 'living water'? Where would that come from, then? Are you greater than our ancestor, Jacob, who gave us this well – and drank from it himself – and his sons and his flocks?" Jesus said, "Whoever drinks the water from this well will

sooner or later become thirsty again; but whoever drinks the water
that I shall give him will never be thirsty again, because that
water will become like a spring inside him, which will give him
eternal life." The woman said, "Then give me some of that water,
sir, so that I shall never be thirsty again – and I shan't have to
keep coming to draw water from this well!" Jesus said, "Go and call
your husband, and come back here." "I have no husband," she
replied. Jesus said "You speak the truth when you say that you
have no husband. You have been married to five men, and the one
you are living with now is not your husband. You certainly told the
truth there." "Sir," she said, "I can see that you are a prophet.

"Our ancestors worshipped God on this mountain; but you Jews
say that God should be worshipped in Jerusalem." Jesus said to her,
"Woman, believe me, the time is coming when you will worship the
Father neither on this mountain nor in Jerusalem. You Samaritans
worship without knowing who it is that you are worshipping – while
the Jews worship whom they know – for salvation comes from the
Jews. But the time is coming – in fact, it's already here – when true
worshippers will worship the Father in Spirit and in Truth. These
are the worshippers the Father wants because he is a Spirit – and
those who worship him must worship him in Spirit and in Truth."
The woman said, "I know that the Messiah is coming, who is called
the Christ. When he comes he will tell us everything." And Jesus
said, "I am he – I who am talking to you."

At that point the disciples returned, and they were very
surprised to find Jesus talking to a Samaritan woman. But no one
said, 'What do you want?' or 'Why are you talking to her?'

The woman left her water jar and went into the town where she
said to the people, "Come and see this man – he told me everything
I ever did! Perhaps he's the Messiah." So they all left the town and
went to the well to see Jesus.

Meanwhile the disciples were trying to get Jesus to eat some of
the food they had brought. But he said, "I have food to eat which
you know nothing about." The disciples were asking each other,
"Has someone already brought him something to eat?" Jesus said,
"No, I mean that it is meat and drink to me to do the will of him
who sent me, until I have finished his work.

J 4:35 "You know how you say: 'Four more months to harvest' – just
look – look at the 'fields.' They are already white – 'ripe for
harvest!' The reaper is drawing his pay – and gathering a crop for
eternal life, so that the sower and the reaper may rejoice together.
The old saying: 'One sows and another reaps' is coming true. I am
sending you to reap a crop for which you haven't worked. Others

have done the work, and you are reaping the harvest of their toil."

While Jesus was telling this to his disciples, the people of Sychar were hurrying to the well. Many already believed in Jesus because of what the woman had said – 'He told me everything I ever did!' When they arrived at the well they begged Jesus to come and stay with them. He stayed in Sychar for two days, and many more came to believe in him because of the words he spoke to them. "We believe in him now," they said to the woman, "not just because of what you said, but because we have heard him ourselves; and we know that he really is the Saviour of the world."

J 4:45   Following those two days at Sychar Jesus went into Galilee; and the Galileans welcomed him because they, too, had been at the Passover Festival, and had seen everything he did there.

Once again he visited Cana-in-Galilee, where he had turned the water into wine; and there he was confronted by a man whose son lay dying in Capernaum. When this man heard that Jesus had come from Judea into Galilee, he came to find him and begged him to come and save his son. Jesus said to him, "Unless you see miracles, you won't believe, will you?" But the nobleman pleaded with him, "Sir, please come, or my son will die." Then Jesus said to him, "It's all right. Go back home. Your son will live." The man believed what Jesus said, and immediately set off on the day's journey home. But before he reached Capernaum, his servants came running to meet him. "He's going to be all right! Your son is going to live!" "When did this happen?" he asked. They replied, "Yesterday. At about one o'clock in the afternoon the fever left him." And the father remembered that it had been at one o'clock that Jesus had told him, 'Your son will live.' He and his household became believers in Jesus.

Mk 1:21
L 4:31   One Sabbath, when Jesus was in Capernaum, he went to the synagogue and began talking to the people. They were all amazed at his teaching because, unlike the Scribes and Pharisees, he spoke with personal authority.

There was a man in the synagogue possessed by an unclean spirit. As Jesus approached, he shrieked, "What do you want with us, Jesus of Nazareth? Have you come to destroy us? I know who you are – the Holy One of God." Jesus rebuked him. "Be quiet!" he said. "And come out of him!" The unclean spirit threw the man into convulsions, and then, with a loud scream, came out of him, leaving him unharmed. The people in the synagogue were astounded. They began to ask one another, "What sort of teaching is this? Did you see the cool way he ordered the spirits about? Yes, and how they obeyed him." The news about Jesus spread like wildfire everywhere in Galilee.

M 8:14
Mk 1:29
L 4:38
•See p. xvii map

They left the synagogue and went straight to Simon and Andrew's house in Bethsaida.* James and John went with them. As soon as they arrived they were met with the news that Simon's mother-in-law was in bed with a high fever. Jesus went in to see her. He took her hand in his and, suddenly, there was no more fever. Jesus helped her to stand – and she began to wait on them.

When evening came, after sunset, everyone in Bethsaida gathered in front of the house. They had brought to Jesus people who were suffering from all kinds of disease; and Jesus laid his hands upon them, one by one, and healed them – so fulfilling Isaiah's prophecy: 'He himself took our illnesses and carried away our afflictions.' He drove out many demons, and he would not let them speak because they knew that he was the Messiah, and many would shout, 'You are the Christ, the Son of God!'

Very early the next morning, long before daybreak, Jesus got up and left the house. He went in search of a quiet place in the countryside outside Bethsaida; and he was praying there when Simon and his friends came to find him. "Everybody's looking for you," Simon said. But Jesus said, "We must go on to other towns. I have to preach to them as well – that is what I came to do." So he went through Galilee, preaching in the synagogues and driving out demons.

M 13.53
Mk 6:1
L 4:16
Isa. 61:1

He came to Nazareth, the town where he had been brought up; and he went to the synagogue, as usual on the Sabbath. He stood up to read the Scripture, and was handed the book of the prophet Isaiah. He opened the scroll and found the passage which reads:

« The Spirit of the Lord is upon me because he hath anointed me.
He has sent me to announce good news to the poor;
To proclaim release for prisoners and recovery of sight for the blind;
To let the broken victims go free;
To proclaim the year of the Lord's favour »

He rolled up the scroll, gave it back to the attendant, and sat down. The eyes of everyone in the synagogue were fixed upon him; and he began to speak to them.

"Today," he said, "in your very hearing, this Scripture has come true." And as they listened to his teaching, the large congregation were amazed by the power and grace of his words.

19

But they said to each other, "Isn't this the carpenter's son? Where did he learn this wisdom – and how is it that he can work these miracles? Mary's his mother, isn't she? Yes, and James and Joses and Simon and Judas are his brothers – and all his sisters are living here. Well then, where has he got all this from?" And they rejected him.

Jesus said, "I'm sure you will quote me the proverb: 'Physician, heal your own.' And you'll say, 'We've heard of all that you have done in Capernaum; do the same here – in your own home town.' Truly, a prophet is respected everywhere but in his own home town and among his own kith and kin.

"I tell you this fact: in Elijah's time, when there was no rain for three and a half years, there was a great famine throughout the land. Although there were many widows in Israel at that time, it was to none of these that Elijah was sent, but to a widow at Sarepta, in Sidon. And there were many lepers in Israel in the time of Elisha, but only one of these was healed – and that was Naaman, the Syrian."

The whole of the synagogue was up in arms at these words. They leapt to their feet and dragged Jesus out of the town to the top of the hill on which the town was built, meaning to push him over the edge. But Jesus walked through the midst of the crowd and left them.

He had been unable to work any miracle there, except that he had put his hands upon a few sick people and healed them; and he marvelled at their lack of belief. "A prophet is not respected in his

J 4:44 own country," he said.

M 14:3 John the Baptist was arrested. Prince Herod had done many evil
Mk 6:17 things, and John had repeatedly warned him that his marriage to
L 3:19 Herodias, the wife of his brother, Philip, was unlawful. Herodias was furious. She wanted John silenced; so Herod crowned all his other misdeeds by having John put in chains and thrown into prison. He would have had him put to death, but he was afraid of popular opinion. The people held that John was a prophet.

M 4:12 When Jesus heard that John had been arrested he settled, not in Nazareth, but in Capernaum. Capernaum is on the Sea of Galilee,
G in the district of Zebulun□ and Naphtali.□ This fulfilled another prophecy: Isaiah speaks of 'the land of Zebulun, the land of
Isa. 9:1 Naphtali, the road by the sea and the land beyond Jordan – Galilee of the Gentiles.' He says, 'The people that lived in darkness have seen a great light; light has shone upon the dwellers in the land of death's dark shadow.'

(M 3:1-2) From that day, Jesus preached the message: "Repent! for the

Mk 4:17
Mk 1:14
L 6:17
M 4:23

Kingdom of Heaven is very close to you." He went all over Galilee teaching in the synagogues, preaching the good news about the Kingdom, and healing many people. His fame soon spread throughout the whole of Syria; and sufferers from all kinds of illness – racked with pain, possessed by devils, epileptic and paralysed, were brought to him, and he healed them all. Many people tried to touch him, for the power was going out of him and healing them. Great crowds followed him – from Galilee, Decapolis (the Ten Towns), from Jerusalem and Judea and from the land on the other side of the Jordan (Perea).

M 8:1
Mk 1:40
L 5:12

Once he was approached by a leper who knelt before him, begging for his help. "If only you will do it," he said, "you can cleanse me." Jesus, filled with pity, reached out to him and touched him. "Indeed I will do it," he said. "Be clean." And at once the leprosy left the man and he was clean. Jesus then spoke sternly to him: "Don't tell anyone about this. Just go and show yourself to the priest, and make the offering required by the Law of Moses for your cleansing. That will certify that you are cured." But the man could not resist telling the whole world about his wonderful miracle. Everywhere he went he told everyone until, in the end, Jesus could not show himself in any town. He stayed in the countryside – and even then, people flocked to him from all directions.

M 9:1
Mk 2:1

When, after some days, he returned to Capernaum, the news flashed round that he was home; and in no time such a crowd gathered that the house was full to overflowing. Soon there was no standing room even in the streets outside the front door.

L 5:17

While Jesus was talking to the people, four men arrived bringing with them a man who was paralysed. They had rigged up a stretcher for him so that they could carry him to Jesus; but when they reached the house the crowds were so great that they could not get anywhere near. Undaunted, they carried him up on to the roof, which they proceeded to dismantle; and when they had made a hole big enough they lowered their friend, stretcher and all, down to the place were Jesus was standing. When he saw their faith, Jesus said to the paralysed man, "Courage, my son! Your sins are forgiven."

M 9:3
Mk 2:6
L 5:21

Some Scribes and Pharisees were present who had come from every town in Galilee and Judea and from Jerusalem. They thought to themselves, "Why does he talk like that? This is blasphemy. Who but God alone can forgive sins?" Jesus knew exactly what they were thinking, and he said to them, "Why do

L 5:24

you harbour such thoughts? Which is easier – to say to this man, 'Your sins are forgiven' – or to say, 'Stand up – and walk'? To prove to you that the Son of Man has power on earth to forgive sins" – he turned to the paralysed man – "I say to you – stand up! Take up your pallet and go home." And the man got up, picked up his 'stretcher' and walked out of the house before them all.

All the people were amazed. Filled with awe, they gave glory to God; and they said, "You'll never believe the marvellous things we've seen here today!"

M 9:9
Mk 2:13
L 5:27

Jesus went back to the shore of Lake Galilee. A crowd gathered round him and he preached to them there. Afterwards, as he was walking along, he came to the customs house; and there he saw Matthew Levi, the son of Alphaeus, sitting in his office. Jesus said to him, "Follow me." Matthew got to his feet and, leaving everything, followed him.

Later, Matthew held a big reception at his house for Jesus. Jesus was seated at table with his disciples, and a large number of tax-collectors and other rough company came and joined them. Some Pharisees and Scribes who were present complained to Jesus' disciples. "Why is it," they said, "that your master eats in such rough company? – these tax-gatherers and sinners." Jesus heard the question and answered, "It's not the healthy who need a

Hosea 6:6

doctor, but the sick. I have come to call not respectable people, but sinners to repentance." And he said, "Go and learn what this text

M 9:14

means: « I require mercy, not sacrifice »"

Mk 2:18
L 5:33

Then they said to him, "Why is it that John's disciples and the disciples of the Pharisees often fast – while yours never do?" Jesus replied, "You don't expect the bridegroom's friends to fast while he is with them. As long as the bridegroom is with them there won't be any fasting. But the time will come when he will be taken away from them. On that day they will fast."

Then he told them another parable: "No one would tear a piece of material from a new cloak to patch an old one, would he? If he did, in the first place he'd have made a hole in his new cloak; and anyway the new material wouldn't match the old cloak.

"And no one puts new wine into old wine-skins because, if he did, the new wine would burst the skins; all of it would be wasted and the skins ruined. You need fresh skins for new wine." He added, "No one wants new wine when they've been drinking the old. They'll say, 'The old is better.'"

M 5:1
L 6:20

One day, when Jesus was followed by a large crowd, he walked up the side of a hill; and when he had sat down, his disciples

L 6:20　　　gathered round him, and he began to teach the people.

G

"Blessed are those who know that they are poor in spirit!" he said. "For the Kingdom of Heaven is theirs.

"Blessed are the mourners – for they shall be comforted.

"Blessed are the gentle – for they shall inherit the earth.

"Blessed are those who hunger and thirst for goodness – their hunger shall be satisfied.

"Blessed are the merciful – for they shall receive mercy.

"Blessed are the pure in heart – for they shall see God.

"Blessed are the peace-makers – for they shall be called the sons of God.

"Blessed are those who have suffered persecution for the sake of goodness; the Kingdom of Heaven is theirs.

"Blessed are you when men hate you and say all kinds of evil things about you for my sake. Celebrate! Be glad about it! For your reward is rich in heaven. That is how they

M 5:13　　　persecuted the prophets before you.

Mk 9:49
L 14:34

"You are the salt of the earth. If salt should lose its taste, what could you ever use to make it taste salty again? It would be fit for nothing except the rubbish heap. Have salt in yourselves and be

M 5:14　　　at peace with one another.

Mk 4:21
L 8:16
L 11:33

"You are the light in the world. Men don't light a lamp – and then put it under a bowl! They put it high – on a stand – so that it lights the whole house. Then you, like the lamp, must shed light among your friends so that, when they see the good you do, they

M 5:17　　　may give praise to your Father in heaven.

"Don't think that I have come to abolish the Law and the Prophets. I have come, not to overthrow them, but to fulfil them. In fact, I tell you, as long as heaven and earth exist, not a letter, not even a dot, will disappear from the Law until every last word has been fulfilled.

"Therefore, anyone who sets aside even the smallest of the commandments, and teaches others to do the same, will rank lower in the Kingdom of Heaven; whereas anyone who keeps the Law and teaches others to do so will be great in the Kingdom of

G

Heaven. And I tell you, unless you obey God's word better than the Scribes and the Pharisees do, you'll never enter the Kingdom of

M 5:21　　　Heaven.

"You have been taught that your forefathers were commanded: 'Thou shalt do no murder. Anyone who commits murder must be brought to judgement.' But I tell you that whoever is angry with his brother without good cause will be brought before the Judge. Whoever calls his brother a good-for-nothing will be brought before the Council; and anyone who calls his brother a worthless fool will be in danger of answering for it in the fires of hell. So – if you are about to offer your gift to God at the altar, and you remember that your brother has something against you, leave your gift there in front of the altar and go at once to make peace with your brother. Then come back and offer your gift to God – because,

L 12:57   if someone sues you, it's better to come to terms with him quickly, before you come to court; for once you are there, he will hand you over to the Judge, who will hand you over to the police, and you will be put in gaol. And there you will stay until you have paid the last farthing of your debt.

"Your fathers were commanded: 'Thou shalt not commit adultery.' But I say to you that if a man looks at a woman with a lustful eye, he has already committed adultery with her in his

M 18:8   heart.

Mk 9:43   "So if your right eye leads you astray, tear it out and throw it away. Better to lose a part of your body than for the whole of it to go to hell. If your right hand is your undoing, cut if off and throw it away. Better

M 19:3 p.68   to lose your right hand than to be dragged with it into hell.

L 16:18   "Your forefathers were told: 'A man can divorce his wife by

M 5:32   writing her a deed of divorce.' But I tell you that if a man divorces his wife for any reason except unchastity, he involves her in

See also   adultery; and anyone who marries her also commits adultery.

M 23:16   "And again, you were taught the commandment: 'Do not break

p. 89   your oath' and 'Oaths sworn to the Lord must be kept.' But I tell

M 5:34   you, you must not swear by any oath – not by heaven: for that is God's throne; nor by earth: for that is his footstool; nor by Jerusalem: for it is the City of the great king; nor even by your own head: because, after all, you can't turn one hair of it white – or black! A plain 'yes' or 'no' is all you need to say. Anything more than that comes from the Evil One.

"You have heard it said: 'An eye for an eye, and a tooth for a

L 6:29   tooth.' But now I tell you: do not take revenge on anyone who does you wrong. If someone hits you on the right cheek, turn and offer him your left. And if someone takes you to court to sue you for your shirt, let him have your coat as well. If anyone forces you to go with him one mile – go with him two miles. Give to everyone who asks you for something; and when someone takes what is yours, do not ask for it back. Do for others what you would want them to do

M 5:43   for you.

L 6:27   "You have heard it said: 'Love your neighbour, hate your enemy.' But now I am telling you: Love your enemies, and pray for those who act spitefully towards you. Only in that way can you become children of your heavenly Father, who makes the sun rise on good and bad alike, and sends rain upon the just and the unjust. Why should you expect any reward if you love only the people who love you? Even tax-collectors do that! And if you are friendly only towards those people who are friendly to you – what's so remarkable about that? Even wicked people do that! And if you lend only to those you know will pay you back – what's the good of that? Even sinners lend to sinners, and expect to be repaid. No – love your enemies and do good to them. Lend and do not look for any return; and you will have a rich reward; you will be the sons of the Most High, because he himself is kind to the ungrateful and wicked. Be merciful just as your Father in heaven is merciful.

M 7:1
L 6:37

"Do not judge others, and you will not be judged. Do not condemn, and you will not be condemned. Forgive others and God will forgive you; because God will judge you in the way that you judge others; and he will apply the same rules as you apply to others, but with greater intensity. Be generous to others, and God will be generous to you – gifts, in good measure – pressed down,

Mk 4.24

shaken together and running over, will be poured into your lap; for whatever measure you deal out to others will be dealt to you in

M 7:3

return.

L 6:41

"Why do you concentrate on the speck of sawdust in your brother's eye – quite oblivious of the plank in your own?! How can you say to your brother, 'My dear brother, let me take that speck out of your eye' – when you can't even see the plank in your own eye? Don't be such a hypocrite! First take the plank out of your own eye – and then perhaps you may be able to see well enough to take the speck out of your brother's eye. And, remember, one blind man can't guide another – they'll both fall into the ditch! Also: a pupil is no cleverer than his teacher; but every pupil, when he has

M 6:19

completed his training, will have reached his teacher's level.

L 12:33

"Don't waste your energies storing up earthly treasure. It'll only get rusty or moth-eaten – or thieves will break in and steal it. Store up treasure in heaven – where no moths will spoil it, and

M 6:24

there aren't any thieves to break in and steal it! For where your

L16:13

treasure is, there your heart will be also. No servant can be a slave to two masters; for he will either hate the first and love the second, or he will be devoted to the first and neglect the second. Just so – you can't love God and money.

M 6:25

"Worrying does no one any good. Is there anyone here who can

L 12:22

add one inch to his height – by worrying about it?! Stop worrying about what you are going to eat, or what you are going to wear.

25

Surely life is more important than food, and the body more than clothes. Look at the lilies of the field – they don't work – they don't spin – yet Solomon in all his glory was not arrayed like one of these! But if this is how God clothes the plants in the fields – which are here today, and tomorrow they're thrown on the fire – will he not all the more clothe you? And look at these wild birds. They don't sow or reap, or store food in barns – yet your heavenly Father feeds them – and you're worth quite a lot more than the birds! How little you trust him! No, don't start worrying about where your food and drink will come from, or your clothes. All these things are for the heathen to run after, not for you – because your heavenly Father knows that you need them. Set your heart first on the Kingdom of God, and on his goodness, and all these things will come to you as well. Don't be anxious about tomorrow – tomorrow will take care of itself. Sufficient unto the day is the evil thereof.

M 6:1
See also
M23:5 p.88

"Take care not to make a great show of your religion to impress your fellow men. You'll receive no reward for that in your Father's house in heaven. When you do some charitable act, for example, don't announce it with a flourish of trumpets, as the hypocrites do, in the synagogues and in the streets, to win everyone's admiration. You've seen what happens; I tell you they've had their reward already. No, when you give to charity, don't let your right hand know what your left hand's doing! Your good deed must be secret, and your Father who sees what is done in secret will reward you.

M 6:5

"And when you pray, don't be like the hypocrites. They love to say their prayers standing up in the synagogue, and at the street corners, so that everyone can see them. I tell you, they've had their reward already. But when you pray, go into your room alone and shut the door, and pray to your Father who is there with you in your secret place; and your Father who knows what you do in secret will reward you. And when you pray, don't keep repeating a lot of meaningless words. The heathen do that, thinking that the more they say the more God will hear them! Don't pray like that. Your Father knows what you want before you ask him. This should be your prayer:

M 6:9
L 11:2

    'Our Father in heaven,
    May your name be kept holy,
    Your Kingdom come,
    Your will be done on earth as it is in heaven.
    Give us today our daily bread.
    Forgive us the wrongs we have done
    As we forgive those who have wronged us.
    Do not bring us to the test,

Mk 11:25	But keep us safe from the evil one.'

"For if you forgive the wrongs others have done to you, your Father in heaven will also forgive you. But if you do not forgive the wrongs of others, then your Father in heaven will not forgive the wrongs you have done.

L 11:5

"Suppose one of you goes to a friend's house in the middle of the night, knocks on the door and says, 'Please lend me three loaves – a friend of mine who is on a journey has just turned up at my house and I haven't a thing to offer him.' And suppose your friend answers from inside the house, 'Go away! The house is all locked up for the night and the children and I are in bed. I can't get up and give you bread at this time of night.' What then? I tell you, even if he won't get up and give you what you want because he is your friend, yet, if you are brazen enough to keep on asking, he will get up and give you everything you need!

L 11:9

"So I say to you: Ask, and you will receive; seek, and you will find; knock, and the door will be opened to you. For everyone who asks will receive, and he who seeks will find; and the door will be opened to anyone who knocks.

M 7:7

"Is there a father among you who would give his son a snake when he asks for a fish? Would you give him a scorpion if he asked for an egg? No matter how bad you are, you know how to give good things to your children. How much more will your Father give the Holy Spirit from heaven to those who ask Him!

M 6:16

"And remember, when you fast, don't go about with a gloomy face as the hypocrites do. They put on a hungry look so that everyone will notice that they are fasting! Well – they've already been paid in full! When you go without food, wash your face and comb your hair so that people don't even know that you are fasting. Your Father, who sees what is hidden, will give you your reward.

M 7:12

"Always treat others as you would like them to treat you. That is the meaning of the Law of Moses and the teaching of the Prophets.

L 6:31

M 7:6

"But do not give what is holy to dogs; and do not give pearls to pigs – they will only trample on them, and then turn and tear you to pieces.

M 7:13

"To get into heaven you have to go in through the narrow gate. The road is easy that leads to hell and the gate is wide, and there are many who travel that road. But the gate is narrow and the way is hard that leads to life, and only a few find it.

L 13:23

M 7:15

"Beware of false prophets. They come to you looking just like sheep – on the outside. But on the inside they are really like wild and savage wolves. You will know them by the way they act. It's

L 6:43

M 12:33

like the fruit on a tree. You don't find grapes on a thorn bush – or figs on thistles! And it's a healthy tree that bears good fruit – a poor tree bears bad fruit. A healthy tree can't bear bad fruit – any more than a bad tree can bear good fruit; and when a tree fails to yield good fruit it is cut down and burned. So look at their fruits – that is how you will know them.

M 7:21

L 6:46

"It's no good to keep calling, me, 'Lord, Lord' if you never do what I tell you. Only those who do the will of my Father will enter the Kingdom of Heaven. When that day comes there are many who will say to me, 'Lord, Lord, didn't we prophesy in your name, and cast out devils in your name, and in your name perform many miracles?' And I will say to them, 'I never knew you. Leave my presence, you and your evil deeds.'

"So now, what about the man who hears these words of mine and acts upon them? He is like the man who was wise enough to build his house upon a rock. The rain poured down, the floods rose, the wind blew and beat upon that house; but it did not fall because its foundations were upon that rock. But what about the man who hears my words but doesn't act upon them? He is like the man who was silly enough to build his house on sand. The rain poured down and the river burst its banks, and the winds blew hard upon that house, and it fell. And what a terrible crash it was too!"

M 7:28

Jesus came to the end of his preaching to the crowds on the hill; and the people were astonished by his teaching because, unlike their own teachers of the Law, he spoke with authority.

M 8:5

L 7:1

When he returned to Capernaum Jesus was met by a small group of Jewish elders. They had been sent to him by a Roman centurion who lived in Capernaum. One of his servants was very ill – in bed, unable to move and in great pain; and the centurion asked if Jesus would come and save his servant's life. The elders approached Jesus and earnestly begged his help. "He well deserves this favour from you," they said. "He has been a good friend to our people; it was he who built our synagogue."

Jesus went with them, but they had not gone far before they were met by some more of the centurion's friends. He had sent them with this message: "Sir, please do not trouble to come to my house; it is not fitting that you should enter it. That is why I did not presume to approach you in person. But if you would just give the order, my servant will get well. I know this because I myself am under orders, and I have soldiers under my command. When I give an order it is obeyed. I say to this man, 'Go', and he goes;

M 8:10

and to that one, 'Come,' and he comes; and I give orders to my servant, 'Do this,' and he does it."

L 7:9

When Jesus heard this he marvelled at the man's faith. He turned to the crowd following him and said, "I tell you, I have never met with faith like this anywhere, even in Israel! Remember my words: a lot of people will be coming from east and west and

L 13:25

will sit down at table in the Kingdom – with Abraham, Isaac and Jacob – while many of those who ought to be in the Kingdom will be thrown into outer darkness, where they will wail and gnash their teeth. Many will try to get in and will be unable, once the master of the House has risen and closed the door; then, when you

See also
M 7:21
p. 28

are standing outside knocking and say, 'Sir, let us in!' he'll answer, 'I don't know where you come from.' And you will answer back, 'Sir, you remember us, we ate and drank with you; you taught in our town!' But he will say again, 'I don't know where you come from. Out of my sight, all of you, you and your evil ways!' And many who are last will be first, and those who are now first will be last."

The messengers went back to the Roman officer's house, and

L 7:11

they found that his good servant had been cured.

On the following day Jesus and his disciples went to Nain (a town in the hills about ten miles south-east of Nazareth). As usual they were followed by a large crowd; and as they approached the town gate they were met by a funeral procession making its way out of the town. It was the funeral of a young man – a widow's only son. Many of the townspeople accompanied the lad's mother; and when Jesus saw her, his heart went out to her "Don't cry any more," he said. Then he stepped forward and laid his hand on the bier, and the men who were carrying it stopped. Jesus said, "Young man, I say to you – get up." The dead man sat up, and began to speak; and Jesus gave him back to his mother. There was an awed silence – then the people were all praising God. "A great prophet has come among us," they said. "God has come to save his people." News of this miracle soon spread through the whole neighbourhood

M 9:35

– and all of Judea.

Jesus went round all the towns and villages, teaching in the synagogues, proclaiming the good news about the Kingdom, and curing all kinds of illness and disease. The sight of the crowds moved him to pity. They were like sheep without a shepherd, anxious and helpless. He said to his disciples, "There is a great harvest, but there are not enough workers to gather it in. You must beg the Owner to send more labourers to harvest his crop."

M 12:1

Mk 2:23
L 6:1

One Sabbath day Jesus was walking through the cornfields. His disciples were with him and, as they went along, they felt hungry; so they started pulling some of the ears of corn, rubbing them in their hands and eating the grain. Some Pharisees saw what they were doing and said to Jesus, "Look at that! Why are your disciples doing what is unlawful on the Sabbath day?" He answered, "And have you never read what David did when he and his men were hungry and had nothing to eat – when Abiathar was High Priest? David ate the shewbread. It is against the Law for anyone, except the priests, to eat those loaves; yet he ate them, and even shared them with his men. And again, you have read, haven't you, that part of the Law which says that on Sabbath days the priests in the Temple break the Sabbath Law – yet it is not held against them? But truly I tell you, there is One here now who is of much more importance than the Temple. And if only you had understood the meaning of the text: « I require mercy, not sacrifice » you would not have condemned the innocent. The Sabbath was made for man – not man for the Sabbath. And the Son of Man is Lord – even of the Sabbath."

1 Sam.
21:3

M 12:7
(M9:13
Hos 6:6)

M 12:9
Mk 3:1
L 6:6

And on another Sabbath day Jesus was teaching in a synagogue, and there happened to be a man in the congregation who had a withered arm. There were also lawyers and Pharisees present, watching and hoping Jesus would do something contrary to the Law so that they could bring a charge against him. "Is it permitted to heal on the Sabbath?" they asked. Jesus knew what was in their minds. He said to them, "Suppose you had a sheep, and it fell into a ditch on the Sabbath. Is there anyone here who wouldn't grab hold of it and haul it out? So then, our Law does allow us to do good on the Sabbath. Well, surely a man is of more value than a sheep!" He said to the man, "Come here and stand by me." Then he turned to his questioners. "Is it permitted to do good or evil on the Sabbath? – to save life – or to kill?" There was no reply. Jesus looked at them. He was angry with them, but also he felt pity – for their stupidity and their harshness of heart. He said to the man, "Stretch out your hand." The man stretched it out – and the withered arm was healed. The Scribes and the Pharisees were furious; and on leaving the synagogue they began plotting against him with some of Herod's men, trying to think of a way to kill him. But Jesus, well aware of what was going on, left that place.

M 12:15

Isa. 42:1

Many followed him, and he healed all who were sick; and he told them all to keep quiet about it. This fulfilled Isaiah's prophecy: "God says « This is my servant whom I have chosen; my Beloved upon whom my favour rests. I will put my Spirit upon him and he will carry true religion to all the nations of the world. He will not make a lot of noise, or make loud speeches in the streets. He will not break the bruised reed, nor will he put out the wavering candle flame. He will bring forth knowledge without pause until he has brought true religion to the earth, and all the people of the earth yearn to do his will »"

Mk 3:20

Jesus went home to Capernaum. Once again such a large crowd gathered round them that they had no time even to eat. When his family heard about this they set out to take charge of him, for

M 12:22

people were saying that he was out of his mind.

Mk 3:22

L 11:14

M 9:32-34

The people brought to Jesus a man who was possessed. He was blind and dumb; and Jesus cured him, restoring both speech and sight. The people were amazed. "Can this be David's son?" they asked. The word went round, but when the Pharisees heard it they said, "He drives out demons only because Beelzebub, the prince of demons, gives him the power to do it." But Jesus, knowing what was in their minds, said, "Any kingdom divided against itself will collapse. No town, or house, that is divided against itself can stand. If Satan were casting out devils, then Satan would be divided against himself. And if it's by Beelzebub that I cast out devils, then by whom do your people drive them out? If that's your argument, your own people will prove you wrong! But if it's by the power of God that I drive out devils, then you can be sure that the Kingdom of God is already here. When a powerful man, fully armed, is on guard over his stronghold, his goods are safe. But when someone stronger than he is attacks and defeats him, he

Mk 9:40

reverse p.29

carries away all the weapons the strong man was relying upon, and divides up all that he has stolen.

M 12:30

L 11:23

"Whoever is not with me is against me; and he who does not gather with me – scatters.

M 12:33

L 6:43

"I have said that you can tell a tree by its fruit. You viper's brood! How can your words be good when your hearts are evil? For the words spoken by the mouth come from whatever fills the heart. A good man, from the treasure in his heart, will speak of good things; while the evil man, from the evil within, will produce evil. I tell you, there is not one thoughtless word that comes from a man's lips but he will have to answer for it on the Day of Judgment. Out of your own mouths you will be acquitted; and out of your own mouths you will be condemned.

M 12:32

Mk 3:30

L 12:10

"Anyone who speaks against the Son of Man can receive forgiveness; but whoever speaks against the Holy Spirit will not be forgiven – now, or ever." Jesus said this because some had said, 'He has an evil spirit in him.'

M 12:38　　At this, some of the doctors of the Law said, "Master, we want
Mk 8:11　　you to show us a sign, to perform a miracle." Jesus sighed deeply;
L 11:29　　then he said, "This is a wicked and perverse generation. It
M 16:1, 4　demands a sign, and the only sign that will be given to it is the
sign of Jonah. Just as Jonah was in the belly of the whale for three
days, so shall the Son of Man be three days in the heart of the
earth.

M 12:41　　"When this generation is on trial at the judgment, the men of
L 11:31　　Nineveh will rise with it, and accuse it; for they repented when
M 12:42　　they heard the teaching of Jonah – and here you have what is
greater than Jonah. And the Queen of the South will complete its
condemnation, for she came from the ends of the earth to hear the
wisdom of Solomon – and what is here is greater than Solomon.

L 11:24　　"When an unclean spirit comes out of a man, it wanders over
the desert looking for a resting place. If it doesn't find one it says to
itself, 'I will go back to the home I left.' And it returns – and finds
the house empty, all tidy and swept clean. Off it goes and brings
along seven other spirits even more wicked than itself, and they all
come in and make themselves at home; and the last state of that
man is worse than the first. That's how it will be with this
generation."

L 11:27　　While he was speaking, a woman in the crowd called out,
"Happy is the womb that bore you, and the breast that suckled
you!" Jesus answered her, "Say, rather, happy are those who hear
the word of God – and abide by it."

M 12:46　　He was still speaking to the crowd when his mother and his
Mk 3:31　　brothers appeared. They stood outside waiting to speak to him.
L 8:19　　Someone said, "Your mother and your brothers are here outside;
they want to speak to you." Jesus replied, "But who are my mother
and my brothers?" (And, looking round at those who were sitting in
the circle about him, he said) "Look! Here (too) are my mother and
my brothers! For whoever does the will of God is my brother, my
M 10:32　　sister, my mother. Whoever will acknowledge me in front of
L 12:8　　everyone will be acknowledged by me before my Father; but
whoever disowns me will be disowned by me.

M 10:40　　"Whoever welcomes one of God's messengers just because he is
Mk 9:41　　God's messenger will be given a reward like his. And whoever
receives a truly good man because he is good will share that
reward. In fact, anyone who gives so much as a cup of water to one
of these children of mine because he is one of my disciples – he will
certainly receive his reward. To receive you is to receive me; and to
receive me is to receive the One who sent me."

Mk 3:7	Jesus and his disciples went away to the shores of Lake Galilee.
M 11:1	Many people followed them from all directions – Galilee, Judea

Jesus and his disciples went away to the shores of Lake Galilee. Many people followed them from all directions – Galilee, Judea and Jerusalem, Idumea and the Transjordan, Tyre and Sidon. They had all heard what Jesus was doing and wanted to see him. Seeing the size of the crowd, Jesus told his disciples to get hold of a small boat for him, so that he would not be overwhelmed by the crowd; for he healed so many that all kinds of sick people were crowding in on all sides trying to touch him. Whenever people with evil spirits saw him they would fall down before him screaming, "You are the Son of God!" But Jesus commanded the spirits not to say who he was.

M 10:1
Mk 3:13
L 6:12
G

In the evening Jesus went off to a hillside to pray. He spent the whole night on the hill praying to God. When daybreak came he called his disciples to him, and he chose twelve of them. He called them his 'apostles' – messengers; and he gave them authority to preach to the people, to drive out evil spirits and to heal all kinds of disease and sickness.

(Nathaniel)

They were: Simon, to whom he gave the name 'Peter,' and his brother, Andrew; James and John, Zebedee's sons – Jesus called them the 'Sons of Thunder!' (Boanerges). There were Philip and Bartholomew, Matthew, the tax-collector, and Thomas; Simon, known as 'the Zealot' (fanatical patriot); James, the son of Alphaeus, and Judas, James' son, also called Thaddaeus, and Judas Iscariot – the betrayer.

M 13:1
Mk 4:1
L 8:4

Another time, Jesus went down to the lake, and as he began to teach, once again a large crowd gathered and he had to get into a boat, where he sat, a few feet from the shore with the whole crowd on the beach, right down to the water's edge. He taught them by parables:

"There was a man who went out to sow his seed," he said, "And it happened that, as he sowed, some seed fell on the footpath; and the birds came and ate it. Some of the seed fell on rocky ground where there was hardly any soil; it sprouted quickly because it was in shallow soil, but at noon, when the sun was really hot, the young seedlings were scorched and, having no proper root, withered away. Some of the seed fell among thistles; and the thistles came up and choked the corn, and it yielded no crop. But some of the seed fell on good soil, and it sprouted and grew, and bore fruit; and the yield was thirty-fold, sixty-fold, and even a hundred-fold. And," he added, "if anyone has ears – let him hear!"

M 13:10

The disciples came to him and said, "Why do you speak to them

Mk 4:10
L 8:9

in parables? And what does this parable mean?" Jesus replied, "You have been given the power of understanding the mysteries of the Kingdom, but to them it is not given. That's why I speak to them in parables; because for all their looking at what is before their very eyes, they can't see it. And for all their listening, they

Isa. 6:9

don't hear or understand. This is the fulfilment of Isaiah's prophecy: « By hearing ye shall hear and shall not understand; and seeing, ye shall see and not perceive; for this people's heart is waxed gross and their ears are dull of hearing, and their eyes they have closed; lest at any time they might see with their eyes and hear with their ears, and might understand with their heart, and

L 10:23

might be converted, and I might heal them » But remember, you are happy men because you can see with your eyes and hear with your ears. I tell you this: many prophets and saints have longed to see what you can see, yet never saw it; and to hear what you can hear, and never heard it."

M 13:18
Mk 4:13
L 8:11

Then he said, "Are you telling me that you don't understand the parable of the sower? Then how are you going to understand any parable? Listen then, and learn the meaning of it. The seed is the Word of God. The seed that fell on the footpath is like the Word sown by God among those who hear it, but then the devil comes and snatches away the Word from their hearts in case they might believe and be saved. The seed sown on rocky ground stands for those who receive the Word with joy when they hear it, but it strikes no root in them; they have no staying power. So when, because of the Word, trouble or persecution comes along, they give up right at the start. And others receive the seed among thistles; they hear the Word, but worldly cares and the false glamour of wealth, and all kinds of bad cravings come in and choke the Word, and it proves barren. But then, the ones who receive the Word in good soil – they hear and understand and accept it, and hold it fast; and because of their steadfastness they bring forth a harvest – some thirty-fold, some sixty-fold and some a hundred-fold."

Mk 4:26

Jesus told them many parables about the Kingdom of Heaven. He said, "The Kingdom of God is like a man who scatters seed in his field. He sleeps at night, he's up and about all day, and all the time the seeds are sprouting and growing. But he doesn't know how it happens. The soil itself makes the plants grow and bear fruit – first the tender stalk appears, then the head, and finally the head full of grain. When the grain is ripe the man gets to work with his sickle, for harvest time has come."

M 13:24   And again, he said, "The Kingdom of Heaven is like a man who sowed his field with good quality seed. But, in the night, when everyone was asleep, an enemy came and sowed weeds among the wheat, and went away. When the corn grew and the ears began to fill out, there were the weeds among the crop. The farmer's men came to him and said, 'Sir, it was good seed you sowed in your field, wasn't it? – then where have all these weeds come from?' The farmer said, 'An enemy has done this.' 'Do you want us to go and pull up the weeds?' they asked. 'No' he replied. 'You might pull up the wheat with them. Let them both grow until harvest; and then I'll tell my reapers, "Gather the weeds first, and tie them in bundles for burning. Then gather the wheat into my barn".' "

M 13:31
Mk 4:30
L 13:18   And he said, "The Kingdom of Heaven is like a mustard seed which a man sows in his garden. Mustard is the smallest of seeds, but when it's full grown it's taller than any other plant. Its branches are so big that birds come and nest in it!" And Jesus also compared the Kingdom of Heaven to yeast. "A woman takes yeast and mixes it with half a hundredweight of flour – and the whole batch of dough rises."

M 13:34
Mk 4:33
Psa. 78:2   Jesus used parables to tell all these things to the crowds all the time; in this way he gave them his message, as much as they were able to receive it. This fulfilled another prophecy: « I will speak in parables. I will tell them things kept secret since the world was made. »

M 13.36   When Jesus had sent the people away and gone into the house, his disciples came to him and said, "Tell us the meaning of the parable about the weeds." Jesus answered, "The man who sowed the seed is the Son of Man; the field is the world; and the good seed stands for the children of the Kingdom. The weeds stand for the children of the evil one. The enemy who sowed the weeds is Satan. The harvest is the end of time, and the reapers are the angels. As the weeds, then, are gathered and burnt, so, at the end of time, the Son of Man will send out his angels, who will gather out of his Kingdom everything that causes offence, and all whose deeds are evil; and these will be thrown into the blazing furnace, the place of wailing and grinding of teeth. And then God's people will shine as brightly as the sun in the Kingdom of their Father.

M 13:47   "Here is another parable: the Kingdom of Heaven is like a net which the fishermen throw out into the lake. It catches all kinds of fish; and when it's full they pull it in and sit down to sort out the fish. The good ones go into their buckets, and the worthless ones are thrown out. At the end of time, in just the same way, the angels will separate the wicked from the good; and the wicked will be thrown into the blazing furnace."

M 13:44　Jesus also said that the Kingdom of Heaven is like a treasure hidden in a field. A man happens to find it and, realising what he has found, he covers it up again and joyfully rushes off to sell all that he owns so that he can go back and buy that field. "Or you could say," he went on, "that it's like a pearl. A buyer comes along looking for fine pearls and he sees one pearl of immense beauty; and he goes and sells everything he has to buy that pearl.

M 13:51　"Do you understand these things?" Jesus asked his disciples. "Yes," they answered. And he said, "This means that every teacher of the Law who becomes a disciple of the Kingdom of Heaven is like a householder who can produce from his store both new things and old.

M 6:22　"Do you ever bring in a lamp and put it under the bed?!" he
Mk 4:21　asked. "You put it on a lamp-stand – so that people can see the
L 11:33　light as they come in. The lamp of your body is your eye. When your eyes are clear your whole body is full of light; but when your eyes are bad, then you are in darkness. Make sure, then, that the light that is in you is not darkness. If your whole body is full of light, with no shadow of darkness, then all will be as bright as if you were under a shining lamp. But if the light in you turns out to
L 12:2　be darkness, how terribly dark that will be! And remember, there is nothing hidden which won't one day be revealed. Whatever is
M 10:26　now concealed will eventually come out into the open.
M 13:12　"Listen carefully to what you are hearing: the measure you give
Mk 4:24　is the measure you will receive, and more. For to the man who has
L 8:18　– more will be given; but the man who has nothing will have taken away from him even the little he thinks he has."

M 8:18　One day, when Jesus and his disciples went down to the lakeside, Jesus, seeing that the lake shore was seriously overcrowded, gave the word to his disciples that they would go to the other side of the lake.

L 9:57　A teacher of the Law came up to Jesus and said, "Master, I will follow you wherever you go." Jesus replied, "Foxes have holes, and birds their nests, but the Son of Man has nowhere to lay his head." And another man, one of his disciples, said, "Lord, let me first go and bury my father." Jesus replied, "Follow me, and leave the dead to bury their dead. You must go and preach the Kingdom of God." Another man said, "I will follow you, sir; but first let me go and say goodbye to my family." Jesus said to him, "No one who sets his hand to the plough and then keeps looking back is any use to the Kingdom of God."

M 8:23
Mk 4:35
L 8:22

Jesus and his disciples then got into a boat and, with several other boats, they set off across the lake. Jesus went to sleep in the stern, his head on a cushion. Suddenly a fierce storm blew up on the lake and, before long, waves were breaking over and filling the boat. The disciples woke Jesus shouting, "Lord! Save us! We're sinking!" He stood up and rebuked the wind and the raging sea – and all was calm. "Why are you so frightened?" he said. "Have you so little faith – even now?" They were filled with wonder. "What sort of man is this," they said, "that even the winds and the sea obey him?"

M 8:28
Mk 5:1
L 8:26

So they came to the other side of the lake, to the country of the Gadarenes, and as Jesus stepped ashore a man came towards him out of the burial caves in the hillside. He had an evil spirit in him, and he lived among the graves. Nobody could keep him in chains any more. He had often been shackled and chained up, but each time he had snapped the chains and broken the shackles. No one was strong enough to master him. And so, unceasingly, day and night, he would cry aloud among the tombs and in the hillsides, cutting himself with stones. When he saw Jesus in the distance, he ran and flung himself down before him shouting, "What do you want with me, Jesus, Son of the Most High God? For God's sake, I beg of you, don't torture me!" For Jesus was already saying to him, "Out! Unclean spirit, come out of this man!" Jesus asked him, "What is your name?" "I am called 'Legion'," he said. "There are so many of us." And he kept asking Jesus not to send 'them' out of the country. Now there happened to be a large herd of pigs grazing on the hillside, and the spirits begged him, "Send us among the pigs and let us go into them." He gave them leave; and the unclean spirits came out of the man and went into the pigs. The whole herd – about two thousand pigs in all – rushed madly down the slope into the water, where they drowned.

The men in charge of the pigs took to their heels. They spread the news of what had happened all the way to Gadara; and everyone came out to see for themselves. They came to Jesus, and they saw the man who had been possessed by devils sitting there – clothed, and in his right mind – and they were afraid. Eye-witnesses told them how the madman had been cured, and what had happened to the pigs. They began to ask Jesus to leave their country.

Mk 5:18

As Jesus was stepping into the boat, the man who had been

L 8:38 possessed pleaded with him. "Let me go with you." But Jesus said, "No. Go home to your own people and tell them what the Lord in his mercy has done for you." The man went off and spread the news throughout all of Decapolis, of all that Jesus had done for him; and everyone who heard it was filled with wonder.

M 9:18
Mk 5:21 As soon as Jesus set foot on the opposite shore, once more a great crowd gathered round him; and while he was still at the lakeside the president of one of the synagogues came up to him. His name was Jairus. He threw himself down at Jesus' feet and entreated him, "My little daughter is dying. I beg you to come and

L 8:40 lay your hands upon her and save her life." So Jesus went with him, followed by the crowd which pressed in upon them so that they could hardly breathe.

M 9:20
Mk 5:25
L 8:43 Among the crowd was a woman who had suffered very badly from a haemorrhage for twelve years. In spite of long treatment by doctors, on which she had spent all the money she had, there had been no improvement; instead she had got worse. She had heard what people were saying about Jesus, so she came up from behind him in the crowd and touched the hem of his robe. "For," she said to herself, "if I just touch his clothes I shall be cured." At once the haemorrhage ceased. She knew that she was cured of her illness. At the same time, Jesus was aware that power had gone out of him. He turned round in the crowd and said, "Who touched me?" His disciples said to him, "Here we are in this jostling crowd, and you ask – who touched you!" Jesus was searching the crowd to see who had touched him; and the woman, trembling with fear when she realised what had happened to her, came and fell at his feet and told him what she had done. He said to her, "My daughter, your faith has cured you. Go in peace, and be healed of your trouble."

While he was still speaking, a messenger arrived from the president's house. "There's no point in troubling the Teacher any further. Your daughter is dead." Jesus heard the message as it was delivered, but he said to the president of the synagogue, "Don't be afraid. Just have faith." After this he allowed no one to accompany him except Peter, James and James' brother, John. They arrived at the president's house where there was a terrible commotion – loud crying and wailing.

Jesus went in and said, "Why all this crying and agitation? The child is not dead; she's only asleep." They all started to laugh at him because they were sure that she was dead. So he turned them all out and, with the child's father and mother and his three companions, he went into the room where the child was lying. Then, taking hold of her hand, he said to her, "Talitha cumi," which means "Get up, little one." At once the little girl got up – and walked about. She was twelve. Her parents were beside themselves with amazement and joy; but Jesus gave strict orders to let no one hear about it. "Give her something to eat," he said.

M 9:27 As Jesus was walking home, two blind men started to follow him. They cried out, "Son of David, have pity on us!" And when Jesus had gone indoors they came to him, and he asked them, "Do you believe that I have the power to do what you ask?" "Yes, sir, we do," they replied. Then he touched their eyes and he said, "As you have believed, so let it be." And their sight was restored. Jesus said to them sternly. "Be sure that no one hears about this." But as soon as they had gone out they talked about him all over the countryside . . .

M 11:2
L 7:18 Word reached John the Baptist, in prison, of what Jesus was doing; and he sent two of his disciples to see Jesus, with the message: "Are you the One John said was to come, or should we expect someone else?" Jesus at that time happened to be healing a large number of sick people – sufferers from diseases and plagues and evil spirits, and they saw him restore sight to several blind
read people. He gave them his answer: "Go and tell John what you
Isa. 35 have seen and heard," he said; "how the blind recover their sight, the lame walk, lepers are cleansed, the deaf hear, and dead men are raised to life. The poor are hearing the good news – and happy is the man who has no doubts about me!"

M 11:7
L 7:24 After John's disciples had left, Jesus spoke to the crowd about him. "When you went out to John in the wilderness, what did you expect to see? A blade of grass bending in the wind? What did you go out to see? A man dressed in fine clothes? You'd need to go to a royal palace for that – to find men gorgeously dressed and living in luxury. Come, tell me, what did you expect to see? A prophet. Yes, And I tell you, you saw much more than a prophet.
Mal. 3:1 For John is the man of whom the Scripture says: « Behold! I will send my messenger, and he shall prepare the way before me. . . » For I tell you there is not a mother's son who is greater than John. And yet the least in the Kingdom of God is greater than he. From the time John preached his message until this very day, the Kingdom of God has suffered violent attacks, and violent men try to seize it. All the prophets, and the Law of Moses, until the time of John, spoke about the Kingdom; and, if you are willing to believe their message, John is Elijah, whose coming was predicted."

L 7:29   When they heard him say this, all the people, including tax-gatherers, praised God, because they had accepted John's baptism. But the Pharisees and lawyers, by refusing his baptism, had rejected God's purposes for themselves.

M 11:16
L 7:31   Jesus went on to say, "Now, how can I describe the people of today? What are they like? They are like children sitting in the market place; and one group shouts to another, 'We played tunes for you, but you wouldn't dance! We sang funeral dirges to you, but you wouldn't cry!' John the Baptist came, and he fasted and drank no wine, and you said, 'He's a madman!' The Son of Man came, and he ate and drank, and you said, 'Look at him! He's a glutton and a wine-tippler; and he's a friend of tax-gatherers and sinners!' And yet God's wisdom is revealed in its truth by all who are its children."

M 11:20
L 10:13   Then Jesus spoke of those towns in which most of his miracles had been performed, and he reproached them because they had not repented of their sins. "Misery and wretchedness lie in store for you, Khorazin!" he said, "And woe to you Bethsaida! For if the miracles that have been performed in you had been performed in Tyre and Sidon, they would have repented long ago in sackcloth and ashes. But no, the day of Judgment will be more bearable for Tyre and Sidon than for you. As for you, Capernaum, do you think you will be lifted up to heaven? No, you will be cast down into hell! For if the miracles which were performed in you had been performed in Sodom, it would still be there today! But the Judgment Day will be more bearable for Sodom than for you."

J 5:1   Jesus went to Jerusalem for one of the religious feasts. Now, in Jerusalem, near the sheep market, there was a pool. In Hebrew it is called Bethesda. It had beside it a colonnade with five arches; and in these arches there lay a large crowd of invalids – blind, lame and paralysed. They were waiting for the water to move. Every now and then an angel of the Lord came down and swirled the water; and the first person who entered the pool after the water had moved was healed of any illness he had. One poor old man had been ailing for thirty-eight years. Jesus saw him lying there and knew just how long he had suffered. "Don't you want to get well?" he said. "Well sir," the man replied, "I don't have anyone to help me get into the pool, you see, when the water's stirred up; and while I'm trying to get in – I'm so slow – somebody else always gets there first." Jesus said to him, "Get up. Pick up your mat, and walk." Instantly the man was cured. He picked up his mat – and walked.

This happened on the Sabbath; and when the Jews noticed the man who had been healed, they said, "This is the Sabbath. You're not allowed to carry your mat on the Sabbath." He said, "The man who cured me said, 'Take up your mat and walk.' " "What man?" they said. "Who told you to pick up your bed and walk?" The man looked wildly about, but there was a big crowd milling around and Jesus was nowhere to be seen. "I don't know who it was . . ." he faltered.

A little later Jesus found him in the Temple. "Now, see, you are well again. Go and sin no more, lest worse befall you." The man left, and went and told the Jews that it was Jesus who had healed him. So then the Jews started to persecute Jesus – for healing people on the Sabbath. But Jesus said to them, "My Father is working all the time – and so am I." That made the Jews angrier than ever, and they plotted even harder to kill Jesus because, they said, not only had he broken the Sabbath but, by calling God 'my Father', he was claiming equality with God.

J 5:19 Jesus answered them, "The truth is that the Son can do nothing on his own – but only what he sees the Father do. What the Father does – the Son does. For the Father loves the Son and shows him all that He Himself is doing; and He will show you greater works than these, which will fill you with wonder. Just as the Father raises the dead back to life – in the same way the Son raises the dead and restores life to them – as he decides. Also the Father does not judge anyone. He has given the jurisdiction to His Son. It is His will that all should pay the same honour to the Son as they do to the Father. Those who deny honour to the Son are denying it to the Father who sent him.

J 5:24 "The plain truth is this: the man who hears my words and believes in Him who sent me – that man has eternal life; and he will not be brought to judgement – he has already moved from death into life. I tell you truly, the time is coming – indeed it is already here – when the dead shall hear the voice of the Son of God; and all those who hear it shall live. For as the Father has life-giving power within Himself, so has the Son – by the Father's gift. And He has given the Son the authority to judge because he is the Son of Man. Do not wonder at this, for the time is coming when all those who are in their graves shall hear His voice, and they shall come forth at His call – those who have done good works, to the resurrection of life; and those who have done evil, to receive condemnation. I cannot act on my own. I judge only as God bids me; so my judgment is just because I follow, not my own will, but the will of Him who sent me.

J 5:31   "A man's testimony on his own behalf is not acceptable. But there is someone else who testifies for me, and I know that his testimony is acceptable; your messengers have been sent to John, and you have his testimony. I have no need of anyone's testimony – I remind you of this for the sake of your own salvation. John was a lamp, burning brightly – and for a time you were glad enough to enjoy his light.

J 5:36   "But I have a witness on my behalf greater than John's: it is the work that I do – the works the Father gave me to do. These speak on my behalf. But you have never heard his voice – you have never seen his face. The Father who sent me speaks on my behalf, but because you have not received his words in your hearts and minds, you will not believe in the One he has sent. You study and study, and search the Scriptures because you think that you will find eternal life in them; and the Scriptures themselves tell you about me – but you will not come to me for life.

    "I do not look to men for honour. But it is different for you, as well I know, because you have no love for God in your hearts. I have come in my Father's name – but you have no welcome for me. If anyone comes to you in his own name – you welcome him! You like to have praise from one another, but you do not try to win praise from the only God. So how can you believe? But don't think that it is I who will accuse you to my Father. It is Moses – in whom you trust – who will accuse you. For if you had believed what Moses said, you would have believed in me. He wrote about me; but since you do not believe what he wrote, how can you possibly believe my words?"

(J 6:1)   Some time later Jesus went back across the Sea of Galilee.

L 7:36   One of the Pharisees invited Jesus to dinner. He went to the Pharisee's house and was seated at the table. There was a woman in that town who was living a sinful life. She heard that Jesus was dining in the Pharisee's house, so she brought an alabaster vessel full of oil of myrrh; and she came and took her place behind him, at his feet, weeping. His feet were wet with her tears, and she wiped them with her hair, and kissed them, and anointed them with the perfume. When his host, the Pharisee, saw this, he said to himself, "If this man really were a prophet he would know who this is who is touching him, and what sort of woman she is." Jesus said to the Pharisee, "I would like a word with you, Simon." Simon said, "Teacher? What is it?" And Jesus said, "There were once two men who owed money to a money-lender. One owed fifty pounds and the other owed five pounds. Neither of them could pay him back, so he cancelled both debts. Now, which do you think would love him the most?" "I suppose," Simon answered, "it would be the one who had owed him the most." "You're quite right, Simon," said Jesus. Then he turned to the woman, and said to Simon, "You see this woman? I came to your house and you gave me no water for my feet; but she has washed my feet with her tears and dried them with her hair. You gave me no kiss of welcome; but she hasn't stopped kissing my feet since I came. You provided no oil for my head; but she has anointed my feet with myrrh . . . And, you see, her great love shows that her many sins have been forgiven. And where little has been forgiven, little love is shown." Then Jesus said to the woman, "Your sins are forgiven." The others said to themselves, "Who is this that he can forgive sins?" But Jesus said to the woman, "Your faith has saved you. Go in peace."

L 8:1 Jesus went through all the towns and villages telling the Good News about the Kingdom of God. The twelve apostles were with him, and also a number of women who had been set free from several ailments and from evil spirits. There were Mary of Magdala (or Magadan – known as Mary Magdalene) from whom seven devils had been cast out; Joanna, the wife of Chusa, an officer of Herod's court; Suzanna, and many others. These women looked after them, and provided food for them at their own expense.

M 10:5 Jesus gave his apostles the authority to cast out evil spirits and to
Mk 6:7 cure every kind of illness and disease. He sent them out with these
L 9:1 instructions: "Don't go into Gentile country or to the Samaritan towns. Go instead to the lost sheep of the house of Israel. Tell them. 'The Kingdom of God is near.' Heal the sick, raise the dead, make lepers clean and drive out demons. You have received without being asked to pay, so now give without asking any return. Don't take any money with you – gold, silver or copper – or anything for the journey; no spare coat or shoes – just a walking stick.

"A worker earns as he goes. When you come to a town or village, seek out some good person who is willing to welcome you, and stay with him until you leave that place. Say, 'Peace to this house,' as you enter it and, if it is a worthy house, your peace will descend upon it; and, if it isn't, then your peace will come back to you. If anyone refuses to receive you or hear what you have to say, leave that house or that town and shake its dust off your feet. This will be a warning to them; for I tell you this – on the Day of Judgment Sodom and Gomorrah will fare better than that place.

L 10:16 "Whoever listens to you, listens to me; whoever rejects you, rejects me; and whoever rejects me, rejects the One who sent me.

M 10:23 When they persecute you in one town, take refuge in another. And, I can tell you, you will not have finished your work in all the towns of Israel before the Son of Man comes.

M 10:24
M 12:24 "No pupil is better than his teacher, is he? – nor a servant greater than his Lord? So the pupil should agree that it's fair to share his teacher's lot, and the servant to share his master's? Well,

(Mk 3:22 if they've called the master 'Beelzebub,' what ever will they call his
p. 31) servants?!

M 10:26 "So don't you be afraid of them. Don't be afraid of anyone who
L 12:4 can kill the body, but cannot kill the soul. I'll tell you whom to fear: fear the One who has the power to destroy both body and soul in hell. Sparrows are two a penny – yet not a single one of them falls to the ground without your Father's leave. As for you – even the hairs of your head are numbered . . . so don't be afraid. You are of more value than quite a few sparrows!

M 10:34 "I came to set the earth on fire – and how I wish that it were
L 12:49 already kindled! I have a baptism to receive – and how tense I am, until it is over! You don't think that I came to bring peace to this earth, do you? I tell you, my coming will bring anything but peace. It is going to set sons against their fathers, daughters against their mothers, young wives against their mothers-in-law. Sometimes a man will find that his worst enemies are under his own roof!

L 14:26 "But no one who puts his mother or father before me is worthy of me. No one is worthy of me who loves his son or his daughter more than me. No one is worthy of me who is not prepared to take up his cross and follow in my footsteps.

"And whoever is concerned about protecting his own life – will lose it. But whoever is ready to risk his life for my sake – will save it. By losing his life for my sake, a man will secure it.

L 14:28 "Would any of you think of building a tower without first sitting down and working out the cost, to see whether you had enough money to finish it? If you got as far as laying the foundations, and then ran out of money – how people would laugh! 'That's the man,' they'd say, 'who started to build – but now he can't finish the job!' Or, what about a king who is planning to go to war against another king. He's not going to march into battle without first sitting down to work out whether he, with his ten thousand men, can hope to engage an enemy who has twenty thousand. If he thought he couldn't, then he'd have to send messengers to meet the king while he was still a long way off – to sue for peace! In the same way, none of you can be disciples of mine without first counting the cost, and being prepared to give up everything for my sake."

Mk 6:12
L 9:6

So Jesus' disciples set out; and they preached to all the people that they must turn away from their sins. They drove out many devils, and they anointed many sick people with oil, and healed them.

M 14:3
Mk 6:17

John the Baptist had told Herod that he had no right to marry his brother's wife, Herodias; and it was due to Herodias' influence that Herod had John arrested and thrown into prison. Herodias nursed a grudge against John and would willingly have had him put to death; but she could not do this because Herod stood in awe of John. He knew him to be a good and holy man. So he just kept John in prison. He liked to listen to him – even though the listening left him greatly perplexed.

Herodias' chance came when Herod gave a banquet on his birthday. He invited all the top government officials, the military commanders and the leading citizens of Galilee. Herodias' daughter, Salome, came in and danced, and she so delighted Herod and his guests that the king said to her, "Ask what you like and you shall have it!" And he swore an oath that he would give her anything she wanted – even if it were half his kingdom. Salome had a word with her mother. "What shall I ask for?" she said. Her mother replied, "The head of John the Baptist." Salome ran back to the king and said, "I want you to give me, here and now, on a big platter, the head of John the Baptist."

Herod was extremely vexed; but because he had sworn an oath to the girl in front of all his guests he could not think how to refuse her. So he sent a soldier of the guard with orders to bring John's head. The soldier went off and beheaded John in prison, and brought the head on a dish, and gave it to Salome. Salome gave it to her mother.

M 14:12
Mk 6:29

When John's disciples heard what had happened they came and took his body away and laid it in a tomb. Then they set out to go and break the news to Jesus.

Mk 6:30
L 9:10
M 14:13

The apostles returned, and came to Jesus with news of all they had been doing: preaching, and healing the people in the towns and villages they had visited.

John's disciples came to tell Jesus of John's martyrdom.

J 6:4

It was almost Passover time. Jesus said to the apostles, "Come with me. Let's go to some quiet place where you can rest awhile." For they had had no time even to eat because there were so many people coming and going. So Jesus and the Twelve started out by

45

boat. But people heard what they were doing; word flew round, and soon people from towns and villages were hurrying over land, round the lake, so that, when Jesus got out of the boat there was a great crowd waiting to greet him. But his heart went out to them, and he began talking to them and teaching them, and he healed all those who were sick.

M 14:15
Mk 6:35
L 9:12
J 6:4

As the day wore on, his disciples came to him and said, "This is a wild and lonely place and it's getting late. We'd better send these people away so that they can go to the nearest farms and villages and get themselves something to eat." "There's no need for them to go," Jesus said. "You give them something to eat." They said, "Do you want us to go and buy twenty pounds' worth of bread to feed this crowd?" "How much bread have you got?" Jesus asked. "Go and see." He said to Philip, "Where can we buy bread to feed all these people?" He said this to test Philip; Jesus himself knew what he meant to do. Philip said, "We could spend a fortune on bread and still not have enough to give each of them even a little bit." One of the apostles, Andrew, Simon's brother said, "There's a boy here who's got five barley loaves and two fish – but what's the good of that among so many?" Jesus said, "Tell them to form groups – and sit down." There was plenty of grass to sit on, and the disciples sat them down in rows of fifty. There were a hundred rows.

Jesus took the five loaves and the two fish, and he looked up to heaven and gave thanks to God. Then he broke the bread and gave it to his disciples, and the disciples gave it to the people. Everyone ate, and everyone had plenty. When they had all eaten enough, Jesus said, "Collect the pieces left over, and let nothing be wasted." And they picked up enough scraps from the barley loaves to fill twelve baskets. Five thousand people ate of those loaves and fishes that day, and that was not counting women and children.

M 14:22
Mk 6:45
J 6:16

When the people saw the miracle Jesus performed, they said, "Surely this is that prophet who was to come into the world." Jesus realised that they were about to carry him off and proclaim him King, so, in the evening he made his disciples get into the boat and go on ahead of him to the other side of the Sea of Galilee, while he himself sent the people away. After saying goodbye to his disciples, he went up the hillside to pray.

As night fell Jesus remained on the hillside, and the boat was well out into the lake; but a strong wind had sprung up and they were being tossed about in choppy water, and not making much headway. Somewhere between three and six o'clock in the morning Jesus, seeing that they were labouring at the oars against a strong headwind, came across the lake, walking on the water. When they saw him walking on the lake they thought he was a ghost, and cried out. They were terrified.

Jesus spoke to them at once. "Take heart!" he said. "It's me; don't be frightened." Peter called to him, "Lord, if it is you, tell me to come to you over the water." "Come," said Jesus. So Peter got out of the boat and stepped down on to the water, and walked towards Jesus. But then – he noticed the strength of the gale, and he was afraid, and he started to sink. He shouted, "Save me, Lord!" Jesus at once reached out and caught hold of him, and said, "Why did you falter? How little faith you have!" Then they climbed into the boat – and the wind died down. The men in the boat fell at his feet and said, "You are truly the Son of God!"

M 14:34
Mk 6:53
They came ashore at Gennesaret, and when the people saw Jesus they sent word to all the sick people in the countryside round about, and brought them to him. They begged him to let them just touch the edge of his robe. And everyone who touched it was completely cured.

J 6:22
The next morning the crowd, which had stayed on the other side of the lake, saw that one of the two boats which had been moored at the lakeside was still at its moorings. They knew that Jesus had not gone in the other boat with his disciples. More boats arrived from Tiberias, near the place where the crowd had eaten the bread and fish after Jesus had broken it. They decided that Jesus and his disciples must all have left, and they took to these boats to go to Capernaum to look for Jesus. When they found him on the other side of the lake they said, "Rabbi! When did you get here then?" Jesus said, "The truth is that you're looking for me, not because of the miracles you have seen, but because your hunger was well satisfied with the loaves you ate! Don't spend all your time working for that sort of food. It's perishable. Work for the food which lasts for ever, which the Son of Man will give you – for God has given him the seal of His authority."

J 6:28
"Then what must we do," they asked, "if we are to work as God would have us work?" And Jesus replied, "The work of God is this: believe in the One he has sent you." So they said, "What sign of power can you give us – so that we can believe? What do you do? Our ancestors were given manna in the desert. The Scriptures say that 'He gave them bread from heaven to eat." Jesus answered, "I tell you truly, the manna Moses gave you was not the real bread from heaven. It is my Father who gives you that. The real bread which God gives is the One who came down from heaven and

brings Life to the world." "Sir," they said, "give us this bread – forever."

Jesus said, "I am that bread of Life. Whoever comes to me will never be hungry, and whoever believes in me will never be thirsty. But, as I have said, you don't believe in me, even though you have seen me. But everyone the Father gives to me will come to me; and whoever comes to me I will never turn away. I have come down from heaven to do, not my own will, but the will of Him who sent me; and it is His will that I should lose none of those He has given me – but raise them up on the Last Day. And this is my Father's will: that everyone who looks upon the Son of Man and believes in him shall have everlasting life."

J 6:35

The Jews took exception to that. They began to whisper to each other about his saying: 'I am the bread which came down from heaven.' They said, "But this man is the son of Joseph, isn't he? We know his father and his mother. So what's he talking about – 'I have come down from heaven'? How can he say he's come down from heaven?" Jesus said, "Don't murmur among yourselves. No one can come to me unless he is drawn by the Father who sent me; and I will raise him up on the Last Day. It is written in the Prophets: « And they shall all be taught by God » Everyone who listens to the Father and learns from him will come to me. I don't mean that anyone, has seen the Father – he who has come from God has seen the Father, and he alone. I tell you truly: the man who believes in me possesses eternal life. I am the bread of life. Your forefathers who ate the manna in the desert – died. But this bread from heaven I'm telling you about is something more. Whoever eats it will not die. I am that living bread which has come down from heaven; and if anyone eats this bread he will live for ever. And the bread which I will give him is my own flesh. I give it – for the life of the world."

J 6:41

J6:46
(J1:18)

The Jews began to argue fiercely about this. "How can this man give us his flesh to eat?" they said. Jesus said, "I tell you, if you do not eat the flesh of the Son of Man, you cannot have life. But whoever eats my flesh and drinks my blood has eternal life, and I will raise him up on the Last Day. My flesh is real food and my blood is real drink. Whoever eats my flesh and drinks my blood lives in me – and I in him. The living Father sent me, and as I live because of the Father, so he who eats me shall live because of me. This is the bread which came down from heaven – and it isn't like the bread which your fathers ate. They are dead; but whoever eats this bread will live for ever."

48

These words were spoken by Jesus when he was teaching in the synagogue in Capernaum.

J 6:60
    When they heard this, many of his followers said, "This teaching is too hard for us. Who can possibly make anything out of that?" Jesus knew without being told what they were saying. "Does that confuse you?" he said. "What if you should see the Son of Man going back to the place he came from?

"It is the Spirit who gives life; the flesh can't do that. My words to you are about the Spirit and the Life; but some of you don't believe them." Jesus knew from the beginning the ones who would believe as well as the ones who would not; and he knew the one who would betray him. He added, "That's why I told you that no one can come to me unless the Father makes it possible for him to do so."

From that time many of his disciples turned back and followed him no more. Jesus said to the Twelve, "And what about you? Do you want to leave too?" Simon Peter answered for them all. "Lord, where would we go? Yours are the words of eternal life. We have faith in you, and we know that you are the Holy One of God." Jesus said, "Have I not chosen you – all twelve of you? - and yet, one of you is a devil." He meant Judas, the son of Simon Iscariot. It was he who would eventually betray him, and he was one of the Twelve.

J 7:1
    After that, Jesus travelled round Galilee. He wanted to stay clear of Judea because the Jews were looking for a chance to kill him.

It was (September) nearly time for the Feast of Tabernacles, and Jesus' brothers said to him, "Why don't you go into Judea? You won't get much publicity in your own home town. If you are really doing these things, let all the world see them." Even Jesus'

Acts 1:14
p. 120
brothers did not believe in him (at that time). He said to them, "The right time for me hasn't yet come; but it doesn't matter when you go. The world can't hate you - but it hates me because I keep telling it about the wickedness of its ways. You go to the Festival. I'm not going yet – because my time hasn't come." Jesus stayed in Galilee, and his brothers went to the Feast. After they had left, Jesus, too, went to Jerusalem – quietly, unnoticed. Everyone seemed to be talking about him, but not openly, for fear of the Jews; and they looked for him at the Festival. "Where is he?" they asked. "He's a good man," said some. Others said, "No he is not. He's leading the people astray."

J 7:14
    About half way through the Festival Jesus went to the Temple, and he began to teach the people. The Jews were very surprised

by his teaching. "How can this man know so much of the Scriptures?" they said to each other. "He's never been a scholar." Jesus said to them, "The teaching I give is not my own; it is the teaching of him who sent me. Anyone who wants to do God's will will know whether my teaching comes from God or not. A person who teaches only his own ideas is seeking glory for himself. But the man who looks for glory to be given to the One who sent him is an honest man and can be trusted to speak the truth.

"Moses gave you the Law – but not one of you obeys the Law. Why are you trying to kill me?" "You're mad!" they said. "Who do you think is trying to kill you?"

Jesus said, "I once performed a great work on the Sabbath; and you were all surprised. Because Moses gave you the law of circumcision – though it originated from the Patriarchs, not Moses – you say that you may circumcise on the Sabbath. So, if a child can be circumcised on the Sabbath without breaking the Law of Moses, why should you be angry with me for giving health to the whole of a man's body on the Sabbath? Do not judge by appearances; judge the truth of things."

J 7:25   Then some of the people in Jerusalem said, "Isn't this the man they're supposed to be trying to kill? Well, look! There he is, speaking to the people as boldly as you like, and no one's saying a word. Do you think the rulers have decided that he is the Messiah after all?" "Yet, wait a minute. We know where this man comes from; and when the Messiah comes, they say, no one will know where he comes from."

Jesus lifted up his voice, and his words rang through the Temple. "You know me? You know where I come from? Yet I haven't come of my own accord. I was sent by the One who is true. You don't know him; but I know him. I came from him – it is he who sent me." Many in the crowd believed him. "When the Messiah comes," they said, "could he possibly do any more mighty works than this man has done?" The Pharisees heard what the people were saying about Jesus, and they and the chief priests sent Temple police to arrest him; but no one could lay hands upon him because his hour had not yet come.

J 7:33   And Jesus said, "I shall be with you for a little longer, then I shall go away – to him who sent me. You will look for me but you won't be able to find me; for where I am going you cannot go." The Jews said to each other, "Where's he going? Where can't we find him? Is he going abroad to teach the Jews living among the Gentiles? Is he going to teach the Greeks?" "He says, 'You'll look for me but you won't find me' and 'You can't go where I shall be.'

What does this mean?"

On the last, most important day of the Festival Jesus stood up in the Temple and spoke loudly and clearly: "If anyone is thirsty, let him come to me. Whoever believes in me, let him drink. The Scripture says to those who believe in me: 'Streams of living water will flow from his heart.' " Jesus was talking about the Holy Spirit which those who believed in him were to receive; but that was to happen after he had been raised to glory. Many people who heard him say this said, "This man really is the prophet." Others said, "He is the Christ." But then others again said, "The Christ is not to come from Galilee. The Scriptures say that the Christ will be a descendant of David's, and he'll be born in Bethlehem, where David lived." So the crowd were divided in their opinions.

Some were all for arresting Jesus, but still no one laid hands on him. The Temple police went back to the chief priests and the Pharisees empty-handed. "Why haven't you brought him?" they demanded; and the officers said, "We've never heard anyone speak the way this man does . . ." The Pharisees were exasperated. "What!" they said. "Have you been deluded as well? Can you name a single one of our rulers who has believed in him? – or one Pharisee? As for this mob in the Temple – they don't know the Law of Moses; so God's curse is on them!"

Then one of their number, Nicodemus, who had once been to see Jesus, said, "According to our Law, we cannot condemn a man without first hearing his defence, and finding out what he has done." "Are you a Galilean too?" they retorted. "Search the Scriptures, and you'll find that no prophets come from Galilee."

J 8:1 Then everyone went home. Jesus went to the Mount of Olives.

J 8:3 Early the next morning he went to the Temple again, and all the people clustered round him; and he sat down and began to teach them. Suddenly, there was a commotion as teachers of the Law and some Pharisees brought in a woman who had been arrested for adultery. They made her stand in the middle, in front of them all. "Rabbi," they said, "this woman was caught in the very act of adultery. The Law of Moses commands that such a woman should be stoned to death. Now what do you say?" They said this to trap him, hoping for an excuse to frame a charge against him. But Jesus was bending down, writing with his finger in the sand, as if he had not heard them. When they kept on asking him he straightened up and said, "Whichever of you has committed no sin, let him cast the first stone." Then he returned to his writing in the sand.

When they heard this, no one spoke; and gradually they all left, one by one, starting with the eldest . . .

Finally Jesus was left alone with the woman – still standing there. He straightened up again and said to her, "Where are they all? Has no one stayed to condemn you?" "No one, sir," she replied. "Neither do I condemn you," he said. "Go, and sin no more."

When Jesus was speaking to the people he said, "I am the Light of the world. No one who follows me will ever walk in the dark – he will have the Light of Life." "That's what you say," the Pharisees said. "You are a witness in your own cause, and that constitutes no proof." Jesus replied, "Even though I am witnessing on my own behalf, my testimony is true, because I know where I come from, and where I am going. You do not know where I come from, or where I am going.

J 8:17   "In your own Law it is written that the testimony of two witnesses is acceptable. Well, here am I – a witness on my own behalf; and my other witness is the Father who sent me." "Where is your father?" they said. Jesus answered, "You know neither me nor my Father. If you knew me, you'd know my Father too. You make your judgments by earthly standards. I am not judging anyone; but, if I did, my judgment would be true because it would not be mine alone, but also of the Father who is with me." Jesus said those words when he was in the Temple treasury, teaching the people; yet still no one arrested him. His hour had not yet come.

J 8:21   And again Jesus said to them, "I shall be going away. You will search for me in vain and you will die weighed down by your sins. Where I am going you cannot come." And the Jews said, "He says that where he is going we cannot come. Does that mean that he's going to kill himself?"

Jesus said to them, "You belong to this world, and I belong to the world above. Your home is here – mine is not. That's why I said that you would die in your sins. For if you do not believe that « I am who I am », you will die in your sins." And they said, "Who are you?" And he replied, "As you have been told from the very beginning. I have much to say about you – and judgements to make of you. But the One who sent me is true, and I am telling the world only what He has told me." They did not understand that he was speaking about the Father. So he said to them, "When you

Ex 3:14	have lifted up the Son of Man you will know that « I am who I am ». Then you will understand that I am doing nothing on my own authority, but that all these things I say to you have been told me by my Father. And he, the One who sent me, is here with me. He has not left me on my own, because I do always those things which please him."
J 8:30	Many who listened to Jesus saying these things believed in him, and to them Jesus said, "If you live by my teaching you really are my disciples; and you will know the truth, and the truth will set you free." "We are the Sons of Abraham," they said, "and slaves to no one. How do you mean – 'we shall be set free'?" Jesus said, "It's nothing but the truth; everyone who sins is a slave. A slave is not one of the family, but the son of the house belongs to it for ever. So, if the Son sets you free, you really are free. I know that you are the children of Abraham – yet you're trying to kill me because you do not accept my teaching. You can't take it in. I'm telling you of what my Father has shown me – and you're doing what you have
J 8:41	learned from your 'father'."

"Abraham is our father," they retorted. But Jesus said, "If you were Abraham's children, you would act like Abraham. Yet here you are – trying to kill me – for telling the truth, as I heard it from God. Abraham wouldn't have done that. No, you are doing as your 'father' does." "We're not baseborn," they answered. "We have only one father – and that is God himself." Jesus said, "But if God were your father, you would love me because I came from the Father. And I didn't come of my own will, either – he sent me. Why is it that you don't understand what I am saying? It's because you can't bear to hear my message. You are indeed the children of your 'father' – the devil – and you naturally follow his ways. From the very beginning he was a killer; and he has never dealt with the truth because there is no truth in him. Lies are natural to him because he's not only a liar, but the father of lies. I tell the truth so you don't believe me. Can any one of you prove that I am wrong? If what I say is true then, why don't you believe me? Anyone who comes from God listens to his words. But you are not God's children, and that is why you aren't listening to me."

The Jews said, "Aren't we right in saying that you are a Samaritan, and that you are mad?" "No. I am not mad," said Jesus. "The truth is that I am honouring my Father, but you dishonour me. In very truth I tell you: anyone who obeys my teaching will never know what it is to die."

The Jews said, "Now we know you're mad. Abraham is dead; the prophets are dead; and yet you say, 'Whoever obeys my

53

teaching will never die.' Our father, Abraham, died. You don't claim to be greater than Abraham, do you? And the prophets also died. Who do you think you are?" Jesus answered, "If I were to honour myself, that would be worth nothing. But my Father honours me – the very One you say is your God, though you don't know him. But I know him; and if I said I didn't I'd be a liar like you! But, in truth, I do know him, and obey his word. Your father, Abraham, was glad to see my day come. He saw it and rejoiced." The Jews said, "You aren't even fifty yet – but you think you've seen Abraham?!" "I tell you truly," said Jesus, "before Abraham was born – « I am »"

Ex 3:14

J 8:59

They gathered stones to throw at him – but then, they could not see him. Jesus walked through the crowd and out of the Temple.

J 9:1

One day, as Jesus was walking with his disciples, they passed a blind man. He had been blind from birth. The disciples said, "Rabbi, whose fault was it that he was born blind? Was it because of his sins, or his parents' sins?" Jesus said, "No. It wasn't because he or his parents sinned. He was born blind so that God's power could be seen at work in him. We must carry out the work of him who sent me while the daylight lasts; soon it will be night, when no man can work. While I am in the world, I am the Light of the world." Then, he spat on the ground and made some mud out of the dust with his spittle, and he spread this mud on the man's eyes. He said to him, "Go and wash in the pool of Siloam" – Siloam means 'sent.' The man went away, and washed, and when he returned, he could see. His neighbours, and people who had often seen him begging for alms said, "Isn't that the man who sat begging?" Some said, "Yes. That's him." Others said, "No. It's not. He just looks like him." So the man said, "It's me. I am the man!" They said, "How were your eyes opened?" and he said, "This man called Jesus made a paste, and he smeared my eyes with it, and then he said, 'Go to Siloam and wash.' And I went, and washed, and as soon as I'd washed – I could see!" "Where is he?" they asked. "I don't know," he said.

J 9:13

They brought the man before the Pharisees. The day when Jesus made the mud and opened the man's eyes was (again) the Sabbath. The Pharisees wanted to know how the man had gained his sight. He told them. "He spread a paste on my eyes," he said. "Then I washed and now – I can see!" Some of the Pharisees said, "Well, obviously the man who did this is not from God, because he doesn't obey the laws of the Sabbath." But others said, "How could a man who is a sinner, though, work such miracles?" They were divided in their opinions. They asked the man: "It was your eyes he opened; what do you say about him?" The man said, "He is a prophet."

The Jews would not believe that the man had been blind and had gained his sight until they called his parents and questioned them. "Is this your son?" they said, "Do you say that he was born blind? Well how is it that he can see now?" "We know that he is our son," they replied; "and we know that he was born blind; but we don't know how he got his sight – or who opened his eyes. He is of age. He can answer for himself – ask him." They said this because they were afraid of the Jews. The Jewish authorities had already ruled that anyone who said that Jesus was the Messiah should be thrown out of the Temple. That is why they said, 'He is of age – ask him.'

For the second time they called the man, and they said to him, "Now, promise before God that you will tell the truth. We know that this man is a sinner." "Whether he's a sinner or not I don't know," the man said. "All I know is that once I was blind, and now I can see." "What did he do to you?" they asked. "How did he open your eyes?" "I've already told you," he replied; "but you didn't take any notice. Why do you want to hear it again? "Do you want to be his disciples too?" They then cursed him. "You are that man's disciple," they said. "We are the disciples of Moses. We know that God spoke to Moses, but as for that fellow – we don't know where he comes from." The man answered, "Well there's a funny thing! Here's a man who's opened my eyes, and you don't know where he comes from? Everybody knows that God doesn't listen to sinners. He listens to people who worship him, and do his will. To open the eyes of a man born blind – no one's ever heard of that. If that man hadn't come from God, he couldn't have done it." "Who do you think you are," they demanded, "to preach to us?! Born and bred in sin, you are." And they threw him out of the synagogue.

J 9:35   Jesus heard that they had thrown him out. When he found him, he said, "Do you have faith in the Son of God?" The man said, "Tell me who he is, sir, so that I can believe in him." Jesus turned to him and answered, "You have already seen him. He is the One who is now speaking to you." "I believe, Lord!" the man said. And he knelt before Jesus.

Jesus said, "I came into the world to judge, so that the blind should see; and to make blind those who see." Some Pharisees who were present said, "Do you mean to say that we are blind?"

Jesus replied, "If only you were blind you would not be guilty. But because you say 'We see', your guilt remains."

J 10:1   "One thing you can be sure of," Jesus said. "If you see a man entering a sheepfold, not by the door, but climbing in some other way – he's nothing but a robber. The man who goes in through the door is the shepherd. The lad who guards the door lets him in, and the sheep hear his voice and know him. He calls his own sheep by name, and leads them out to pasture. And when he has brought them all out, he goes ahead, and the sheep all follow him, because they know his voice. They won't follow anyone else. They'll run away from a stranger, because they don't know his voice."

Jesus told them this parable, but they did not understand it. So Jesus said, "The meaning of those words is that I am the door for the sheep. The sheep took no notice of anyone who came before me, for these were all thieves and robbers. But I am the door. Whoever comes in through me will be safe. He shall go out and come in, and he will find good pasture. The thief comes only to steal, kill and destroy. But I have come so that men may have

J 10:11   life – and have it to the full. I am the good shepherd; and a good shepherd is ready to die for his sheep. A hired hand, when he sees a wolf coming, makes himself scarce to save his own skin. He abandons the sheep, and the wolf catches them, and scatters the flock. Well – the hired hand is no shepherd, and the sheep aren't his, and he doesn't care.

"I am the good shepherd; I know my sheep; and my sheep know me – just as I know the Father, and he knows me. I am willing to die for my sheep. There are other sheep too, who belong to me – not of this sheepfold; and I must bring them in; and they too will know my voice. Then there will be one flock and one shepherd.

"The Father loves me because I am laying down my life, so that I may receive it back again. No one is taking it from me. I am laying it down of my own free will. I have the power to lay it down, and the power to take it again. This is by the commandment of my Father."

These words caused argument and division among the Jews. Many of them were saying, "He's possessed! He's mad! Why listen to him?" Others were saying, "No. A man possessed by an evil spirit doesn't talk like that." – and – "Could an evil spirit open a blind man's eyes?"

J 10:22   It was winter in Jerusalem, and the time of the Festival of Dedication. Jesus was walking in the Temple in Solomon's Cloister. The Jews gathered round him and said, "How long are you going to keep us guessing? If you are the Christ, say so plainly." Jesus said to them, "I have told you so already, but you do not believe it. My credentials are the works I do in my Father's name; but because you are not sheep belonging to my Father's flock, you don't believe. My own sheep hear my voice; I know them, and they follow me. I give them eternal life, and they shall never die; and no one can steal them away from me. And my Father who has given them to me is greater than all, and no one is going to steal them from his care; and the Father and I are one."

J 10:31   Again the Jews picked up stones to throw at him. At this, Jesus said, "I have shown you many good works; for which of these would you stone me?" "We're not about to stone you for any good deed," they said, "but for blasphemy. You are only a man, but you are trying to claim to be a god." Jesus answered, "But even so, you cannot, by the Scriptures, charge me with blasphemy; for is it not written in your own Law that God said « Ye are gods »? The Scriptures are true for ever. Those are called gods to whom God's message was given. So why do you charge me with blasphemy? – because, I, consecrated and sent into the world by the Father, said « I am God's son »? If I am not doing my Father's work, do not believe me. But if I am, you should at least believe in my actions, so that you may know once and for all that the Father is in me, and I am in the Father."

Once again they tried to arrest him, but he evaded them and slipped away. And he went back again across the Jordan to the place where John had been baptising, and stayed there. Crowds of people came to see him. "John didn't perform any miracles," they said, "but everything he said about this man was true." And many of the people there believed in him.

M 15:1
Mk 7:1   A group of Pharisees and doctors of the Law who had come from Jerusalem, met Jesus; and they noticed that some of his disciples were eating their food with 'defiled' hands – in other words, without first performing the Jewish ritual washing ceremony. For none of the Jews will eat unless they have first washed their hands and arms to the elbow, in obedience to the tradition of the elders. They will not eat any food bought at the market without first washing it; and they have to keep a number of other traditions about washing jugs and cups and basins, and

beds. So these Pharisees and lawyers asked him, "Why do your disciples not conform to the ancient tradition, but eat their food with defiled hands?" Jesus answered them, "How right Isaiah was when he prophesised about you! You are hypocrites – just as he wrote: '« These people » says God « honour me with words, but their hearts are far from me. But they worship me in vain because

Isa. 29:13   they teach man-made commandments as though they were God's commands »' You neglect God's commandments," he said, "and enforce the teachings of men."

And Jesus continued, "You have clever ways of rejecting God's laws in order to promote your own teachings. For Moses said,

Mk7:9   'Honour thy father and thy mother' and 'the man who curses his father and his mother must suffer death.' But you teach that a man has only to say to his parents, 'This money of mine might have been used for your benefit, but it is "Corban"' – which means: "set apart for God" – then he is not allowed to use it to help his father and his mother! Thus, by your own tradition which you have taught to others, you have made God's word ineffective. And there are many similar things that you do."

Then Jesus called the crowd to him once more, and he said, "Listen to me, all of you, and understand this: nothing that goes

M 15:10   into a man from outside can defile him. No, it's what comes out of a
Mk 7:14   man's mouth that can make him unclean."

When he had left the people and gone indoors his disciples questioned him about this parable. Jesus said, "Do you mean to

M 15:15   say that you don't understand it either? Don't you see? – anything
Mk 7:17   which goes into a man's mouth passes into his stomach and then on out of his body. But the things which come out of the mouth come from the heart – bad thoughts which can lead him to kill, commit adultery, and do other immoral things – to rob, lie, and slander people. Those are the things which can defile a man. But to eat without washing your hands according to ritual practice – that can't defile anyone."

The disciples said, "Do you know that the Pharisees have taken great offence at the things you have been saying?" Jesus replied,

M 15:12   "Every plant which has not been planted by my heavenly Father will be rooted up. Don't worry about them. They are blind guides; and when one blind man guides another, they both fall into the ditch."

Jesus then withdrew from that part of the country to a place near Tyre and Sidon. He found a house to stay in and hoped that

M 15:21   no one would know he was there. But it was impossible to stay
Mk 7:24   hidden. Almost as soon as he arrived a foreign woman whose

daughter was possessed by an evil spirit heard about Jesus, and came to him at once and fell at his feet. This woman was a Gentile – a Syro-Phoenician by birth. She begged him to drive the evil spirit out of her daughter. But Jesus answered, "Let us feed the children first. It is not right to 'take the children's bread and throw it to the dogs.' " "That's true sir," she said; "but even the dogs eat the scraps that fall from the master's table!" Jesus said to her, "For those words you may go home content. You are a woman of great faith. What you have asked will be done." The woman returned home, and found her daughter lying calmly in bed. The evil spirit had left her.

Mk 7:31   On his way home from the neighbourhood of Tyre, after going by way of Sidon, Jesus made a detour through the Ten Towns (Decapolis) where some people brought him to a man who was deaf and had a speech impediment; and begged him to lay his hands on him. Jesus took the man away from the crowd, and he put his fingers into the man's ears; then he wetted his finger with saliva and touched the man's tongue; and, looking up to heaven, with a deep sigh, he said "Ephphatha!" – which means: 'Open!' The man's ears were opened, his tongue was freed from its impediment and he could speak as well as the next man. Jesus forbade them to tell anyone; but the more he forbade them, the more they told everyone. They were all completely amazed, and they said, "How wonderful are all the things he has done! He even makes the deaf hear, and the dumb speak!"

M 14:1   Now everyone was talking about Jesus, and the news reached
Mk 6:14   Herod. Some people were saying, "John the Baptist has come
L 9:7   back to life! That's why he has these miraculous powers." Others said, "He is Elijah." And others said, "He is a prophet, like one of the old prophets." When Herod heard all this, he said, "It's John; I had his head cut off, and he has come back to life." And he kept trying to see Jesus.

M 15:29   After leaving Decapolis Jesus took the road by the Sea of Galilee and went up into the hills. When he was seated there, crowds came flocking to him, bringing with them the lame, blind, dumb and crippled, and many other sufferers. They placed them at Jesus' feet, and he healed them. The people were full of joyful amazement when they saw the dumb speaking, the crippled strong, the lame walking, and sight restored to the blind; and they praised the God of Israel.

M 15:32
Mk 8:1

Jesus called his disciples to him. "I feel sorry for these people," he said. "They have been with me for three days, and now they have no food. I don't want to send them away in case they faint on the road home. Many have come a long way." The disciples said, "Where can we find enough food to feed them all in a deserted spot like this?" How many loaves have you?" Jesus asked. "Seven," they replied. "And there are a few small fish." So Jesus made all the people sit down on the ground; then he took the loaves and the fish and, after giving thanks to God, he broke them and gave them to the disciples, and the disciples gave them to the people. They all ate, and all had plenty to eat; and this time the disciples took up seven baskets of leftover pieces. There were about four thousand people, not counting women and children. Jesus sent the crowds away and got into a boat, and went into the countryside near Magadan.

M 16:1
Mk 8:11
L 12:54
(M 12:38
L 11:29
p. 32)

Some Pharisees and Sadduces came to see Jesus, and they started to argue with him. To put him to the test they asked him for a sign from heaven. But Jesus, with a deep sigh, said, "When the sun is setting you say, 'The sky is red, it'll be a fine day tomorrow' – and it is. And early in the morning you say, 'The sky is red, it's going to rain" – and it does. You can forecast the weather by looking at the sky; how is it that you can't interpret this fateful hour? You ask me for a sign. The only sign that will be given to this wicked generation is the sign of Jonah."

M 16:5
Mk 8:13

L 12:1

With that he left them, returned to the boat, and started out to cross to the other side of the lake. The disciples had forgotten to bring any extra bread for the journey across the lake, and they had only one loaf with them in the boat. (Remembering his conversation with the Pharisees) Jesus said to them, "Be very careful! You must be on your guard against the yeast of the Pharisees and the Sadduces." The disciples (preoccupied with their concern about the lack of bread) said to each other, "He's talking about leaven! – it's because we haven't got enough bread!" Jesus said, "What are you talking about – not having brought enough bread? Don't you understand what I am saying? Can't you see with your eyes, or hear with your ears? Don't you remember the five loaves for the five thousand, and how many baskets full of leftover pieces you picked up? Or the seven loaves for the four thousand and how many basketsful you picked up? How can you fail to see that I'm not talking about bread 'Be on your guard,' I said, 'against the yeast of the Pharisees and the Sadduces.' " Then they understood. They were to be on their guard, not against the baker's yeast of the Pharisees and Sadduces, but against the leaven of their teaching and their hypocrisy.

They arrived in Bethsaida; and the people there brought along a blind man and asked Jesus to touch him. Jesus took the blind man

Mk 8:22   by the hand and led him out of the village. Then he spat on the man's eyes and laid his hands on him, and asked him, "Can you see anything?" The man said, "I can see men, moving about – but they look like trees walking about." Jesus laid his hands on his eyes again. This time the man stared straight in front of him. His sight was perfectly restored and he could see everything clearly. Jesus said to him, "Go home now; but don't go back to the village, or tell anyone about this."

Jesus and his disciples set out for the village of Caesarea Philippi. On the way Jesus asked them, "Who do people say that I

M 16:13   am?" They answered, "Some say you are John the Baptist; others
Mk 8:27   say you are Elijah, and others say you are Jeremiah, or one of the
L 9:18   other prophets." "And you," he said, "Who do you say that I am?" Simon Peter answered, "You are the Messiah, the Son of the living God." Then Jesus said, "Simon, son of Jonah, you are a happy man indeed! For this truth did not come to you from any human source, but it was given to you directly by my heavenly Father. And I say to you, Simon-bar-Jonah, you are Peter – the Rock; and on this rock I will build my Church; and even the forces of death

J 1:42   shall never prevail against it. I will give you the keys to the
p. 12   Kingdom of Heaven. Whatever you forbid on earth shall be forbidden in heaven; and whatever you allow on earth, shall be

(M 18:18   allowed in heaven." Then Jesus commanded his disciples to tell no
p. 66)   one that he was the Messiah.

From that time onward Jesus began to make it clear to his disciples that he had to go to Jerusalem and there to suffer much at the hands of the elders and the chief priests and the teachers of the Law. He would be put to death, and he would be raised from

M 16:21   death on the third day. When Peter heard him say this, he took
Mk 8:31   him aside and began to chide him. "God forbid it, Lord! This shall
L 9:22   never happen to you!" But Jesus turned to Peter and said, "Away with you, Satan! You are a stumbling block to me. You're thinking

see also   as men think – not as God thinks."
pp. 63, 78

Then he turned to his disciples. "Remember," he said, "that anyone who wants to follow me must forget himself. He must take up his cross and come with me. The man who wishes to save his own life will lose it; but the man who would lose his life for my sake will find it. What would a man gain by winning the whole world if, in the process, he lost his true self? Or what could he give that would buy that true self back? For the Son of Man is to come in the glory of his Father with His angels, and then he will give each man his due reward for what he has done. I tell you this: there are some here today who will not taste death before they have seen the Son of Man coming in his Kingdom."

Mk 9::1

M 17:1

Mk 9:2

L 9:28

About a week later, Jesus went up into the hills to pray. He took Peter, James and John with him. He led them up a high mountain where they were quite alone.

While Jesus was praying his disciples went to sleep; and as he prayed he was transfigured. His face changed in appearance, and it shone like the sun. And his clothes became as bright as light.

Peter and his companions woke up to see Jesus standing there in his glory; and in this heavenly radiance they saw two men standing there with him. They were Moses and Elijah, and they were speaking to him about his destiny in Jerusalem and his departure from this earth. The disciples were dazed by the brilliance and, as the two men left Jesus, Peter said, "Master, how good it is to be here! Shall we make three tabernacles – one for you, one for Moses, and one for Elijah?" He did not really know what he was saying – and even as he spoke, a bright cloud appeared, and hung over them; and as it advanced and surrounded them they were very frightened indeed. A voice spoke from the cloud: « This is my own dear son. Listen to him. » On hearing the voice the disciples were so terrified that they threw themselves face downward on the ground. Then Jesus came and touched them. "Stand up," he said, "Don't be afraid." And when they raised their eyes, they saw no one but Jesus – alone.

Mk 9:9

As they came down from the mountain Jesus said, "Don't tell anyone what you have seen until after the Son of Man has been raised from death." The disciples kept his command and at that time told no one of anything they had seen; but they discussed among themselves what this 'raised from death' might mean. They asked Jesus, "How is it that the teachers of the Law say that first Elijah must come?" He replied, "Yes, Elijah does come first, to set everything right. But I tell you Elijah has come already – and they didn't recognise him; and they have worked their will upon him. And the Son of Man is going to suffer at their hands in the same

M 17:10

M 17:14
Mk 9:14
L 9:37

way." The disciples realised that Jesus was talking about John the Baptist.

The following day, when they came down from the mountain and returned to the rest of the disciples, they found that a large crowd had gathered round them and some Scribes were arguing with them. As soon as the crowd realised that Jesus was there, an awed silence fell; and then they ran to greet him. Jesus asked what all the argument was about. A man stepped forward from the crowd and said, "Master, look at my son, I beg you – my only child. He's an epileptic, and his fits are very bad. He shrieks, and falls down; and he grinds his teeth and goes rigid, and shakes violently – he's often badly bruised. I brought him to your disciples, but they couldn't heal him." Jesus answered, "What an unbelieving and perverse generation this is! How long shall I be with you and have to bear with you? Bring your son here to me." But before the boy could reach him, the evil spirit dashed him to the ground where he lay, foaming at the mouth, and in convulsions. "How long has he been like this?" Jesus asked the father. "Ever since he was a child," he replied. "Many a time it's nearly killed him, throwing him into the fire – or into the water. If it is at all possible for you, take pity on us and help us." "If it is possible!" Jesus said. "All things are possible to a man who has faith." "I have faith," the father said (with tears in his eyes). "Only help me – when my faith is weak." Then Jesus, seeing that the crowd was closing in on them, sternly rebuked the unclean spirit. "Deaf and dumb spirit," he said, "I command you to come out of him, and never return." The spirit screamed, and threw the boy into another fit; and then it left him. He lay still as death. In fact, many said, "He's dead." But Jesus took his hand and raised him to his feet, and gave him back to his father. And all the people were amazed at the mighty power of God.

L 9:43
M 17:19
Mk 9:28
L 17:5

When Jesus had gone indoors, the disciples asked him privately, "Why couldn't we drive the evil spirit out?" Jesus answered, "It was because your faith was too weak. I tell you, if you have faith no bigger even than a mustard seed, you have only to say to this mountain, 'Move – from here – to there!' and it will move. Nothing would be impossible for you. However, there is no way to cast out this sort of spirit except by prayer and fasting."

M 17:22
Mk 9:30
L 9:44
See also
pp 61, 78

They now left the district and journeyed together round Galilee. Jesus wanted no one to know where they were because he was teaching his disciples. For the second time, he said to them, "The Son of Man will soon be given up into the power of men. They will kill him but on the third day after he is killed, he will rise again from the dead." They were deeply distressed. They did not know what his words meant, and they were afraid to ask him.

M 17:24

As they entered Capernaum the Temple tax-collectors came up to Peter and they asked, "Does your master pay Temple tax?" "Yes," said Peter, "he does." Peter went into the house to see Jesus, and Jesus spoke first. "What do you think, Simon – from whom do the kings of this world collect taxes – from their own citizens – or from aliens?" "From aliens," Peter replied. "Well then" said Jesus, "that means that the citizens are exempt. But we don't want to cause trouble with these people, so go and cast a line in the lake. Take the first fish that comes to the hook, open its mouth, and you will find a silver coin. Take that and pay them our taxes – it will be enough for both of us".

M 18:1
Mk 9:33
L 9:46
Mk 10:15

As they went indoors, Jesus asked them, "What were you arguing about as we were coming along the road?" No one spoke, because on the road they had been arguing about who among them was the greatest. Jesus sat down and called the Twelve to him. "Whoever wants to be first," he said "must put himself last, and be servant of all." He took a child and stood him in front of them all, and put his arm round him. "Remember this," he said: "unless you change and become like little children, you

L 18:17

will never enter the Kingdom of Heaven. Let a man humble himself until he is like this child, and he will be the greatest in the Kingdom of Heaven. The person who, in my name, welcomes one of these little ones welcomes me; and whoever welcomes me welcomes not only me, but the One who sent me."

L 9:49
Mk 9:38
(p. 31
reverse
M 12:30)
M 10:42

John said to him, "Master, we saw a man driving out devils in your name; but he wasn't one of us, and we tried to stop him." Jesus said, "Don't stop him. No one who does a work of divine power in my name will be able in the same breath to speak evil of me. For anyone who is not against us is on our side. Remember, anyone who gives you so much as a cup of water because you are followers of the Messiah, that man will surely not go unrewarded.

M 18:6
Mk 9:42
L 17:1

"As for the man who leads astray one of these little ones who believe in me, it would be better for him that he should tie a milestone round his neck, and be cast into the depths of the sea, than for him to cause one of these children to turn away from me. Alas for the world that such causes of stumbling arise! Come they must, but woe betide the man through whom they come! Never despise one of these little ones, I tell you, they have their guardian angels in heaven, who look continually on the face of my Father."

L 15:1   Another time, tax-gatherers and other bad characters were all
crowding in to listen to Jesus; and the Pharisees and doctors of the
Law began muttering to each other, "This man mixes with bad
company – he even eats with them!" So Jesus told them a parable:

M 18:12   "If one of you has a hundred sheep, and loses one of them," he said,
"doesn't he leave the ninety-nine grazing on the hillside and go
after the lost one until he has found it? And how does he feel when
he's found it? He lays it across his shoulders, and he goes gladly
home and calls his friends and neighbours together. 'Come and
celebrate with me!' he says. 'I've found my lost sheep!' In the same
way, I can tell you, there will be greater joy in heaven over one
sinner who repents, than over ninety-nine people who are so good
that they have no need to repent.

G
L 15:8   "Or again, suppose a woman has ten pieces of silver and loses
one of them. Doesn't she light the lamp and sweep out the house
and look in every corner until she has found it? And when she's
found it, she calls all her friends and neighbours together and says,
'Come and celebrate with me! I've found the piece I lost!' In the
same way, I tell you, there is joy among the angels of God over one
sinner who repents."

L 15:11   And he told them another parable: "There was once a man who
had two sons; and the younger son said to his father, 'Father, give
me my share of the estate now.' So the father divided the property
between his two sons.

"A few days later the younger son sold his share and left home
with the money. He went off to a foreign country and spent it all,
down to the last farthing, on wild parties and reckless living. Then
a severe famine spread over that country, and he was left utterly
penniless. So he went to work for one of the local landowners who
sent him out to tend the pigs on his farm. He was so hungry that
he would have been glad to eat the pig food; but no one gave him
anything.

"Finally he came to his senses. 'There are goodness knows how
many hired men on my father's farm who have more food than
they can eat,' he said; 'and here am I – starving to death! I will set
off and go back to my father. I'll say to him, "Father, I've behaved
very badly. I've offended against God and against you; and I'm no
longer fit to be called your son. Only let me be like one of your
hired men." ' And forthwith he got up and started off on the
journey home to his father.

"He was still a long way from home when his father saw him;
and his heart went out to him in pity. He ran to meet him,

flung his arms around him and kissed him. The son said to him, 'Father, I have sinned – against God and against you; and I'm no longer worthy to be called your son. Just treat me like one of your hired servants.' But the father said to his servants, 'Quickly! Bring a robe – the best one – and put it on him. Put a ring on his finger and shoes on his feet. Then bring the fatted calf and kill it, and let's have a big feast to celebrate this day! For here's this son of mine; he was dead, and now he's alive again; he was lost, and now he is found!' And the festivities began.

"Now the elder son had been out in the fields all day. On his way back, as he came near the house, he heard music and dancing. He called out to one of the servants and asked what was going on. The servant said, 'Your brother has come home, and your father has killed the fatted calf because he has got him back safe and sound.' This made the elder brother so angry that he would not go into the house. His father came out and begged him to come in; but he replied, 'Look, for years I have worked like a slave for you. I never once disobeyed an order of yours, and yet you never gave me so much as a kid for a feast with my friends. But now this son of yours turns up after squandering all your money on prostitutes, and you kill the fatted calf for him.' 'My son,' said the father, 'you are always with me, and everything I have is yours. It's right that we should have a celebration feast today, because your brother was dead and has come back to life; he was lost – and is found.'"

M 18:15

And Jesus said, "If your brother commits a sin against you, go and tell him his fault. But do it privately, just between yourselves. If he repents, forgive him – you have won your brother over. If he won't listen, take one or two people with you so that 'every accusation can be upheld by the evidence of two or three witnesses.' If he won't listen to them either, then take the whole matter to the church; and if he won't listen even to the church, then you'll have to treat him as you would a pagan, or a tax-collector.

M 18:18
M 16:19
p. 61

"And I tell you: whatever you forbid on earth shall be forbidden in heaven; and whatever you allow on earth shall be allowed in heaven. Also I tell you that whenever two or more of you agree about anything you pray for, it will be done for you by my Father in heaven. For where two or three meet together in my name, I am there with them."

M 18:21
L 17:3

Peter came to Jesus. "Lord, how many times can my brother sin against me and I have to forgive him, then?" he said. "As many as seven times?" "No, not seven times," Jesus replied. "Seventy times seven. If he sins against you seven times in one day and comes to you saying that he's sorry, you must forgive him.

M 18:23   "The Kingdom of Heaven is like this," he said. "There was once a king who decided to settle up his accounts with the men who served him. Right at the start one of them was brought before him whose debt ran into millions. He had no way of paying the debt, so the king ordered him to be sold as a slave, and his wife and children and all that he had, to pay the debt. The servant flung himself down at his master's feet. 'Just give me a little time,' he begged, 'and I'll pay you everything.' The king was so sorry for him that he let the man go, and cancelled his debt. But as soon as the man went out he came across one of his fellow servants who owed him a few pounds. He caught hold of him and grabbed him by the throat and said, 'Pay me what you owe me.' The other man fell at his feet and begged him, 'Just give me a little time and I will pay you.' But he refused, and had him thrown into prison until he had paid the debt.

"When the other servants saw what had happened, they were deeply distressed; and they went to the king and told him the whole story. So the king sent for his servant. 'You scoundrel!' he said. 'I forgave you the whole of your debt when you appealed to me. Should you not also have had pity on your fellow servant just as I had pity on you?' And the king was so angry that he sent the servant to prison to undergo torture until he had repaid the debt in full. And that is how my heavenly Father will deal with you, unless each one of you forgives his brother from his heart."

L 10:1
L 9:1
p. 43

M 10:16

The Lord appointed a further seventy-two disciples to be sent on ahead, in pairs, to every town and place he was going to visit. He spoke to them as he had to the Twelve when he first sent them out: "The crop is heavy," he said, "and the harvesters are few. Pray therefore to the Owner of the harvest that he send more labourers to harvest the crop. Off you go. Look, I am sending you out like sheep among wolves. You must be as wary as serpents and as harmless as doves. Don't take any purse or knapsack or shoes; and don't stop to greet anyone on the road. When you go into a house let your first words be: 'Peace to this house!' If there is a man of peace there, your peace will rest on him; if not, it will return and rest on you. Stay in that one house, eating and drinking whatever they provide – for the labourer is worthy of his pay; don't move from house to house. When you come to a town and they make you welcome, eat the food provided for you; heal the sick there, and tell them: 'The Kingdom of God has come close to you.' But if

M 10:14
L 10:11

you come to a town where they don't make you welcome, go out into the streets and say, 'The very dust of your town that clings to our feet we wipe off, to your shame. But remember this: the Kingdom of God has come close to you.' I tell you, it will be more bearable for Sodom on the Great Day than for that town."

M 19:1
Mk 10:1

Then Jesus left Galilee and went into Judea, where he crossed the River Jordan. Great crowds followed him, and he healed them and taught them as he always did.

M 19:3
L 16:18
(M 5:32
p. 24)

Gen. 2:24

Some Pharisees came to see him and tried to trap him with crafty questions. "Is it lawful," they asked, "for a man to divorce his wife for any and every reason?" Jesus replied with a question. "Haven't you ever read this Scripture: 'In the beginning the Creator made them male and female; and he said « For this reason a man will leave his father and mother, and be made one with his wife, and the two shall be one flesh »'? It follows, then, that they are no longer two, but one. What God has joined together, man must not separate."

"But why, then," they objected, "did Moses rule that a man might divorce his wife by giving her notice of divorce and sending her away?" Jesus replied, "It was because you were so hard to teach that Moses gave you permission to divorce your wives; but it was not like that in the beginning. I tell you, if a man divorces his wife for any reason except unfaithfulness, and marries another woman, he is committing adultery; and in the same way, a woman who divorces her husband and marries another man commits adultery."

M 19:10

The disciples said to him, "If that's how it is between a man and his wife, it's better not to marry at all." To this Jesus replied, "That is something which not everyone can accept – only those for whom God has ordained it. There are several reasons why a man cannot marry: some are incapable of marriage because they were born so, or they were made so by men; there are others who have themselves renounced marriage for the sake of the Kingdom of Heaven. Let those accept it who can."

M 19:13
Mk 10:13
L 18:15

Some people brought their little children, even their babies, to Jesus for him to lay his hands on them and pray. The disciples scolded them for doing this, but when Jesus saw what they were doing, he was vexed. He called the children to him, and he said, "No, don't try to stop them. Let the children come to me; for the Kingdom of Heaven belongs to such as these." Then he took the children in his arms, and laid his hands on each of them, and blessed them. And he went on his way.

M 19:16
Mk 10:17
L 18: 18

As he was leaving, a young Jewish leader ran up to him and knelt before him. "Good master," he said, "what must I do to receive eternal life?" "Why are you calling me good?" Jesus asked. "No one is good except God alone. But, if you want life, keep the commandments." "Which commandments?" asked the man. Jesus answered, "Do no murder; do not commit adultery; do not steal; do not give false evidence; honour your father and your mother; and love your neighbour as yourself." The young man answered, "But master, I have kept all these commandments since I was a boy." Jesus looked straight at him, and his heart warmed towards him. He said, "There is one thing you lack: go and sell everything you have and give to the poor; and you will have riches in heaven; and come and follow me." At these words the man's face fell; and he went away with a heavy heart, for he was a very

M 19:23
Mk 10:23
L18:24 G

wealthy man.

Jesus looked at his disciples and said, "How hard it will be for wealthy people to enter the Kingdom of God!" They were amazed to hear him say this; but he insisted, "Children, it is so hard for those who trust in riches to enter the Kingdom of God. It's easier for a

G

camel to pass through the eye of a needle than for a rich man to enter the Kingdom of God." They were even more amazed, and said to each other, "Then who can be saved?" Jesus looked at them, and he said, "For men it is impossible. But with God all things are possible."

M 19:27
Mk 10:28
L 18:28

Then Peter said, "Well, we've left everything to become your disciples." And Jesus said, "Yes. And I tell you, when the Son of Man sits upon his glorious throne in the world to come, then you twelve followers of mine will also sit on thrones, to judge the twelve tribes of Israel.

"Everyone who has given up home, brothers or sisters, mother, father, children – or land – for my sake, and for the Gospel's, will receive in this age a hundred times as much – houses, brothers, sisters, mothers and children, and land – and persecutions as well! – and in the world to come – eternal life. But many who are first will be last, and the last first.

M 20:1

"The Kingdom of Heaven," he said, "is like this: There was once a landowner who went early one morning to the market place to hire labourers to work in his vineyard; and after agreeing to pay them the going rate (1 denarius per day) he sent them off to work. He went to the market place again at nine o'clock and saw others standing idle. "Go and join the men working in my vineyard,' he said, 'and I will pay you a fair wage.' So off they went. At noon he went out again, and at three in the afternoon, and made the same arrangement as before. It was an hour before sunset when he went out again to the market place and found another group standing there. 'Why are you standing about like this all day doing nothing?' he asked. 'Because no one hired us,' they replied. So he told them to go and join the others in the vineyard.

"Evening came, and the landlord said to his foreman, 'Call the labourers and give them their pay, beginning with those who were hired last, and ending with the first.' Those who had started an hour before sunset came forward, and each was paid one silver denarius. But when the men who had been hired first came to be paid, they took the money, grumbling against their employer. 'You've put these newcomers on the same level as us,' they said; 'and they've only worked for an hour. But we have sweated the whole day long in the blazing sun.' The owner turned to one of them and said, 'Listen friend. I haven't cheated you. You agreed to work the whole day for a denarius, didn't you? Now take your pay and go home. If I choose to give this man who was hired last the same as you, don't I have the right to do as I wish with my own money? Or are you jealous simply because I am generous to him? Just so, those who are last will be first, and those who are first will be last."

L 10:17
The seventy-two came back, jubilant. "Lord," they said, "even the demons obeyed us when we commanded them in your name!" Jesus answered, "Yes. I saw Satan fall, like lightning, from heaven. Indeed, I have given you the power to tread underfoot snakes and scorpions and all the forces of the enemy. Nothing shall injure you. But – don't feel glad just because the evil spirits obey you. Rather be glad because your names are written in heaven."

M 11:25
L 10:21
In that hour, Jesus thrilled with joy in the Holy Spirit; and he said. "Oh Father! Lord of Heaven and Earth! I thank you for hiding these things from the learned and wise, and showing them to simple men. Yes, indeed, Father. That was how you wanted it to be." To his disciples he said, "Everything is entrusted to me by my Father; and no one knows who the Son is except the Father – or who the Father is, but the Son, and those to whom the Son may choose to reveal him."

M 13:16
L 10:23
Then, turning to his disciples, he said to them privately, "How happy you are to see the things you are seeing! As I've told you, many prophets and kings have longed to see what you see, but they couldn't – and to hear what you hear, but they never did.

M 11:28
"Come unto me all of you who are tired of carrying your heavy burdens," he said, "and I will give you rest. Take my yoke upon

70

you and learn from me; for I am gentle and humble in heart; and you will find rest for your souls. My yoke is easy and my burden is light."

L 10:25 On one occasion a teacher of the Law came to Jesus to ask a trick question. "Teacher," he said, "what must I do to inherit eternal life?" Jesus answered, "What do the Scriptures say? What is your reading of it?" The man replied, " 'Love the Lord your God with all your heart, with all your soul, with all your strength, and with all your mind; and your neighbour as yourself.' " "That's right," said Jesus. "Do that and you will live." Eager to justify himself, the lawyer persisted. "But who is my neighbour?" he said.

And Jesus replied, "A man was on his way from Jerusalem to Jericho when he was attacked by robbers, who stripped him, and beat him, and left him there – half dead. It so happened that a priest was going down the same road. When he saw the wounded man, he crossed the road, and went past on the other side. So did a Levite who came along. He went and had a look at him, but then he passed by on the other side. But a certain Samaritan who was making the same journey, came upon him; and when he saw him, his heart was filled with pity. He went over to him and bandaged up his wounds, bathing them with oil and wine; and he set him on his own beast, and took him to an inn where he looked after him. And the following day he took out two silver coins and gave them to the inn-keeper. 'Take care of him,' he said; 'and if you spend more than that I'll repay you on my way back.' Which of these three men, do you think, was neighbour to the man who fell among thieves?" "The man who took pity on him," the lawyer replied. Jesus said, "Then go and do the same."

L 10:38 As Jesus and his disciples went on their way, they came to a village where a woman named Martha made him welcome in her home. She had a sister, Mary, who sat at Jesus' feet, and stayed listening to his words. Martha was so busy with all the housework and cooking that she became quite distracted; and she came to Jesus and said, "Lord, don't you care that my sister has left me to cope with all this work on my own? Tell her to come and give me a hand." But the Lord answered, "Martha! Martha! You are caring and worrying about so many things. But only one thing is really important – and Mary has chosen it. It'll not be taken away from her."

L 11:37 A Pharisee invited Jesus to eat with him. When he went in and

See also
p. 89
M 23:25

sat down to eat, the Pharisee was surprised to see that Jesus did not perform the ritual washing ceremony beforehand. So the Lord said to him, "You Pharisees! You clean the outside of the cup and plate, but your lives are full of greed and malice. Foolish men! Did not God, who made the outside, also make the inside? But give what is in your cups to the poor – and cleanse what is on the inside, and then nothing will be unclean."

L 11:53

When Jesus left the house, the lawyers and Pharisees began to criticise him fiercely; and they cross-questioned him on many points, hoping to trap him into saying something which was contrary to the Scriptures.

L 12:13

A man in the crowd said, "Teacher, tell my brother to give me my share of our inheritance." Jesus replied, "Man, who made me judge or arbitrator over your affairs?" Then he turned to the people who stood beside him and said, "Beware! Be on your guard against greed of every kind; and remember, no matter how rich a man may be, his life is not a part of his possessions." And he told them this parable:

"There was once a man whose land yielded good crops. He debated with himself: "What am I to do? I haven't enough room to store all my produce.' Then he said, 'I know what I'll do – I'll tear down these store-houses and build bigger ones. I'll collect all my corn and my possessions and store them. Then I can really say to myself, "Man, you've plenty of good things laid by – enough for many a year. Take it easy! Eat, drink and enjoy yourself!"' But God said to him, « Foolish man! This very night your soul will be required of you. You have spent all this time collecting all this stuff – and who will have it now? » So it is with the man who piles up riches for himself. In God's sight he's nothing but a very poor man."

L 12:32

To his disciples Jesus said, "Don't be afraid, little flock! For your Father has chosen to give you the Kingdom. Sell all your possessions and give your money to the poor. Provide yourselves with purses that won't wear out, and store up riches in heaven. They won't depreciate there! No thief can get near them and no moth will destroy them! For where your wealth is, there your heart will be too.

"Be ready for action, with belts fastened and lamps lit. Be like men awaiting their master's return from a wedding party, ready to let him in the moment he knocks at the door. Blessed are those servants whose master finds them awake and ready when he comes! I tell you, he'll buckle his belt, sit them down at the table and come and wait on them. Even if he should come as late as midnight – or even later – how happy they are if he finds them

M 24:43 ready! You may be sure that, if a householder knew at what time the thief was coming, he'd keep watch and stop him breaking in. So you too, must always be ready, because the Son of Man will be coming at a time when you least expect him."

M 24:45
L 12:41 Peter said, "Lord, do you mean this parable for us, or is it for everyone?" The Lord said, "Well, who is that faithful and wise servant? He's the one the master will put in charge, to 'run the household', and to give the other servants their 'share of the food' at the proper time. Oh, how happy is that servant if he's found hard at work when his master comes! I tell you, he'll be put in charge of all his master's property. But if the servant says to himself, 'The master's a long time coming;' and begins to bully the menservants and maids, and to eat and drink and get drunk, then the master will arrive on a day when the servant's not expecting him, at a time he doesn't know; and he'll punish him severely – and he'll be assigned the fate of the disobedient.

L 12:47 "The servant who knows his master's wishes but makes no attempt to carry them out will be beaten severely. But one who doesn't know his master's wishes, and has earned a beating, will be flogged less severely. The man to whom much is given – of him much is required. The man to whom more is given – of him much more is required."

L 13:1 It was at this time that some people came to Jesus and told him about the Galileans, whose blood Pilate had mingled with their sacrifices. He answered them, "Do you think that, because these Galileans suffered this fate, they must have been greater sinners than anyone else in Galilee? I tell you, they were not. What about the eighteen people who were killed when the tower fell on them at Siloam – do you think they must have been worse sinners than all the people living in Jerusalem? No. I tell you, they were not. – But, unless you repent of your sins and turn from them, you will suffer the same fate."

L 13:6 Then Jesus told them this parable: "A man had a fig tree growing in his vineyard. He came looking for fruit on it – but there was none. So he turned to the gardener. 'Look here,' he said. 'For the last three years I've been looking for fruit on this tree and there has been none at all. Cut it down. Why should it go on taking up good space in the soil?' But the gardener said, 'Leave it, sir, just one more year, and I'll dig round it and feed the soil a bit; and if it bears fruit next season, all well and good; and if it doesn't, then have it cut down.' "

L 13:10 One Sabbath Jesus was teaching in a synagogue, and there was a woman present who suffered from an evil spirit in her which had crippled her for eighteen years. In fact, she was bent double, and could not straighten herself up at all. When Jesus saw her he called to her, "Woman, you are freed from your affliction." He laid his hands upon her shoulders and at once she stood straight; and she began to praise God. But the president of the synagogue was affronted because Jesus had healed her on the Sabbath; and he said to the people. "There are six working days. Come and be cured on one of them, and not on the Sabbath." The Lord said, "You hypocrites! Is there a single one of you who doesn't untie his donkey or his cow from the stall and take it out for a drink of water on the Sabbath? And here's this woman, a daughter of Abraham, who has been kept prisoner by Satan for eighteen long years. Was it wrong for her to be untied from her bonds on the Sabbath?" At his words, his opponents were covered with shame. But the people were delighted with all the wonderful things Jesus was doing.

L 14:1 On another Sabbath Jesus went to eat a meal at the house of a leading Pharisee, and from the moment he entered the house the Pharisees were watching him like hawks. And there, in front of him, was a man with dropsy. Jesus asked the lawyers and Pharisees, "Does the Law allow healing on the Sabbath, or not?" They said not a word. So he took the man and healed him, and sent him away. Then he turned to them and said. "If one of you had a cow or a donkey, and it fell into a well on the Sabbath, would you hesitate to pull it out?" But they were unable to answer that question either.

L 14:7 He noticed that all the guests were trying to sit in the best places at table; and he told them a parable: "When you are invited to a wedding," he said, "don't sit down in the place of honour. It may well be that a more distinguished guest than yourself has been invited. And the host will come to you and say, 'I'm afraid you'll have to give this man your seat.' Then how silly you'll look as you make your way to the lowest place at the table! No, when you receive an invitation, go and sit in the lowest place; and then, when he comes, your host may say, 'Come and sit higher up the table, my friend!' Then you will be honoured before your fellow guests. For everyone who exalts himself shall be humbled; and whoever humbles himself will be exalted."

L 14:12 Then he said to his host, "When you give a dinner party, don't just invite your friends or brothers, or other relations, or rich neighbours. They'll only ask you back again, and then you'll be repaid. When you give a party ask the poor, the crippled, the lame and the blind; and so you will find happiness. For you see, they have no means of repaying you. But you will be repaid – on the Day when good men rise from the dead."

L 14:15
(M 22:1 on a different occasion)

One of the assembled company said, "Happy is the man who shall sit at the feast in the Kingdom of God!" Jesus answered, "A man was giving a big dinner party, and he invited a lot of people. When all was ready he sent out his servants with a message for his guests: 'Please come; everything is now ready.' But they all began, one after the other, to make excuses. The first said, 'I've just bought a piece of land, and I have to go and see it. Please accept my apologies.' The second said, 'I have bought five pairs of oxen and I am just on my way to try them out. Please accept my apologies.' Another said, 'I've just got married. I'm sorry I can't come.' The servant came back and reported all this to his master. The master of the house was very angry. 'Go out quickly,' he said, 'into the streets and alleys of the town, and bring me the poor, the blind, the crippled and the lame.' Then, later, the servant said, 'Sir, your orders have been carried out, and still there is room.' The master said, 'Go out into the highways and the byways and make them come in. I want my house to be full. I tell you – not one of those who were invited shall taste my banquet.' "

L 16:1

Jesus said to his disciples: "There was once a rich man who employed a steward to manage his estate. He received reports that this steward was squandering his master's money; so he sent for the man and said, 'What's this I hear? Hand over your accounts to me, for you can no longer be my steward.' The steward said to himself, 'What shall I do? I'm about to lose my job; I'm not strong enough to dig ditches, and I'm too proud to beg . . .' Then he said, 'I know what I must do so that, when I leave here, there will be people who will offer me a house and home.' He summoned his master's debtors, one by one. To the first he said, 'How much do you owe my master?' He replied, 'A thousand gallons of oil.' 'Here's your account,' said the steward. 'Sit down and write five hundred; be quick.' Then he said to another, 'And you, how much do you owe?' 'A thousand bushels of wheat,' he said. 'Take your account,' said the steward, 'and make it eight hundred.' And the master praised the steward for his astuteness. 'For the people of this world,' he said, are much more shrewd in the handling of their affairs than are the people of the light.'

L 16:9

"So I say to you," said Jesus, "use your worldly wealth to win friends for yourselves so that, when money is a thing of the past, you may be received into an eternal home; (for friendships are of eternal value).

"The man who can be trusted in small things can also be trusted in great things. If, then, you have not proved trustworthy with what belongs to another, who will ever give you what is yours?

"And you know that no servant can be the slave of two masters. Either he will hate the first and love the second; or he will be devoted to the first and think nothing of the second. You can't serve God and money."

The Pharisees, who loved money, heard all this – and scoffed. He said to them, "You are the people who impress your fellow men with your righteousness. But God sees through you. For what the world thinks of great value is of no value at all in the sight of God.

"The Law and the prophets lasted until John came. Since then the Good News of the Kingdom of God has been preached; and now everyone is trying to push in. It would be easier for heaven and earth to pass away than for one iota of the Law to lose its force."

L 16:19

And another time he said, "There was once a rich man who dressed himself in purple and the finest linen; and he feasted in great magnificence every day. At his gates there lay a poor man named Lazarus. He was covered with sores, and he'd have been glad to ease his hunger with the scraps from the rich man's table. And dogs would even come and lick his sores. One day the poor man died and was carried away by the angels to be with Abraham. The rich man also died and was buried; and in Hades, being in torment, he looked up; and far away he saw Abraham with Lazarus close beside him. 'Abraham, my father!' he called out. 'Have pity on me! Send Lazarus to dip his finger in some water to cool my tongue, for I am in torment in this fire.' But Abraham said, 'Remember, my son, that all the good things came to you in your lifetime, and all the bad to Lazarus. Now he is receiving consolation here and it is you who are in agony. But that is not all. There is a great chasm fixed between us; no one from our side who wants to reach you can cross it, and none may pass from your side to us.' 'Then, father,' he said, 'will you send him to my father's house, where I have five brothers – to warn them, so that they too do not come to this place of torment?' But Abraham said, 'They have Moses and the Prophets; don't they listen to them?' 'No, father Abraham,' he replied; 'but if someone from the dead visits them, they will repent.' Abraham answered, 'If they do not listen to Moses and the Prophets, they will pay no heed – even if anyone should rise from the dead.' "

L 17:7   Jesus said to his disciples, 'Suppose one of you has a servant ploughing, or minding sheep. When he comes back from the fields, will you, the master, say to him, 'Come along at once and sit down and eat'? Is the master expected to be grateful to the servant for carrying out his orders? Will he not more likely say to him, 'Now: go and get my supper; make yourself tidy and wait on me while I eat. Then you can have yours afterwards.'? So with you. When you have carried out all your orders, you should say, 'We are servants; we deserve no credit because we have done no more than our duty.' "

On his way to Jerusalem, Jesus was travelling through the borderlands of Samaria and Galilee; and as he was coming into one of the villages there, he was met by ten men who had leprosy. They stood some way off and called to him, "Jesus! Master! Have pity on us!" When he saw them he said, "Go, and show yourselves to the priests." And while they were on their way they were made clean. One of them, when he saw that he was healed, came back, shouting praises to God. He threw himself at Jesus' feet, thanking him. He was a Samaritan. Then Jesus said, "Weren't all ten cleansed? The other nine — where are they? Could none be found to come back and praise God – but only this stranger?" And he said to the man, "Get up, and go on your way. Your faith has made you well."

L 17:20   Some Pharisees asked Jesus when the Kingdom of God would come. He replied, "The Kingdom of God does not come – in such a way as to be seen. No one will say, 'Look! Here it is!' or 'There it is!' – because the Kingdom of God is within you."

L 18:1   Jesus told his disciples a parable about the need always to be praying and never to lose heart. "In a certain town," he said, "there was a judge who had no reverence for God; and he had no respect for men either. And in that same town there was a widow who kept coming to him demanding justice. 'Justice against my opponent!' was her appeal. The judge didn't want to know about this case, but after a while he said to himself, 'Even though I don't fear God, and have no respect for men, yet because of all the trouble this widow is giving me, I will see to it that she gets her rights – before she wears me out with her badgering!' " And the Lord said, "You hear what that unjust judge said? Now, will not

God judge in favour of his people who cry to him for help day and night? Will he be slow to help them? I tell you, he'll judge in their favour, and quickly . . . But will the Son of Man find faith on earth when he comes?"

L 18:9 He also told this parable to people who were so sure of their own goodness, and looked down on everyone else: "Two men went into the Temple to pray – one a Pharisee and the other a tax-collector. The Pharisee stood apart, by himself, and prayed: 'I thank you, God, that I am not greedy or dishonest, or immoral – or, for that matter, like that tax-collector over there. I fast two days every week, and I give you one tenth of all my income.' But the tax-collector stood at a distance, and would not even raise his eyes to heaven, but beat upon his breast, and said, 'O God! Be merciful to me, sinner that I am!' I tell you," said Jesus, "it was this man and not the other, who had put himself right with God when he went home. For everyone who has a high opinion of himself will be humbled, and the truly humble will be exalted."

L 9:51 As the time drew near when Jesus was to be taken up into heaven, he set his face resolutely towards Jerusalem. He sent messengers ahead to make arrangements, but when they arrived at a Samaritan village the villagers would not receive him because it was plain that he was on his way to Jerusalem. When the apostles, James and John (the 'Sons of Thunder') heard this they said, "Lord, may we call down fire from heaven to consume them, as Elijah did?" But he turned and rebuked them. "You don't know what Spirit you represent," he said. "The Son of Man hasn't come to destroy men's lives, but to save them." And they went on to another village.

M 20:17
Mk 10:32
L 18:31
See also
pp. 61, 63
They were on the road to Jerusalem; Jesus was leading the way. The apostles following him were filled with apprehension, and the disciples who followed miserably behind them were afraid. Jesus took the Twelve aside and, for the third time, he spoke to them of what was going to happen to him. "We are now going to Jerusalem," he said, "and everything the Prophets wrote about me will come true. The Son of Man will be given up to the chief priests and the doctors of the Law. They will condemn him to death and hand him over to the Gentiles. He will be mocked and spat upon, flogged and killed. And three days after that he will be raised to life." The disciples did not understand any of these things; the meaning of the words was hidden from them, and they did not know what Jesus was talking about.

L 13:31 A number of Pharisees came to him and said, "You should get out of here and go somewhere else, for Herod wants to kill you." Jesus replied. "Go and tell that fox: 'Today and tomorrow I shall be casting out devils and healing people; on the third day I shall finish my task.' But I must journey on today, tomorrow and the next day, because it is unthinkable that a prophet should be killed anywhere else but in Jerusalem . . .".

M 20:20
Mk 10:35

The mother of Zebedee's sons (James and John) came before him with her sons. She bowed low and asked a favour of him. "What is it you wish?" asked Jesus; and she answered, "Promise me that when you come into your Kingdom my two sons here may sit next to you, one on your right and the other on your left." Jesus turned to the brothers and said, "You don't understand what you're asking. Can you drink the cup that I am to drink? Can you be baptised in the way that I am to be baptised?" "We can," they replied. Then he said to them, "You shall indeed share my cup, and be baptised in the way I am to be baptised. But permission to sit at my right hand and my left is not for me to grant. These places belong to those for whom my Father has prepared them."

M 20:24
Mk 10:41

When the other disciples heard about this they were indignant with the two brothers. So Jesus called them to him and he said, "You know that the world's rulers lord it over their subjects, and how powerful leaders use their authority over them. But this is not the way it's to be with you. Among you, whoever wants to be great must be willing to be the servant of you all; and whoever would be first must be willing to be everyone's slave – like the Son of Man. He did not come to be served, but to serve; and to surrender his life as a ransom for many."

Mk 10:46
L 18:35
(M 20:
29-34)

As he approached Jericho a blind man was sitting at the roadside, begging. He was Bartimaeus, the son of Timaeus. Hearing the crowd going past, he asked what was happening. "Jesus of Nazareth is passing by," they told him. He shouted out, "Jesus, Son of David! Have pity on me!" The people in front of him told him sharply to be quiet, but he shouted even more loudly, "Son of David, have pity on me!" Jesus stopped and told them to bring him forward. "It's all right, " they said. "He's calling you." He threw off his cloak and came to Jesus. "What do you want me to do for you?" Jesus asked him. "Lord," he said, "that you would give me back my sight . . ." "Go your way," Jesus said. "Your faith has healed you." And immediately the man's sight was restored; and he followed Jesus, praising God. And all the people gave praise to God for what they had seen.

L 19:1   Jesus went on to Jericho and, as he was walking through the city, crowds gathered to see him. There was a man there called Zacchaeus, who was a tax-superintendent, a very rich man. He wanted very much to see what Jesus looked like; but he could not see him at all because of the crowd. He was a little man. So he ran ahead and climbed a sycamore tree on Jesus' route so that he could get a good look at him as he passed by. When Jesus came to the tree, he looked up and saw him. "Zacchaeus, make haste and come down," he said. "I am coming to stay at your house today!" Zacchaeus climbed down as fast as he could and gladly welcomed Jesus. When they heard this the crowd started to grumble that Jesus was going to be 'a guest in the house of a sinner.' But Zacchaeus stood there and said to the Lord, "Here and now, Lord, I give half my possessions to the poor. And if I have cheated anyone, I will pay him back four times as much." Jesus said, "Today salvation has come to this house! – for this man, too,

M18.11   is a son of Abraham, and the Son of Man came to seek and save the lost." And he went on to tell them a parable – because he was now nearing Jerusalem, and they thought that the reign of God was suddenly to come into view at any moment . . .

M 25:14   "A certain nobleman went into a far country to receive for
L 19:12   himself a kingdom, and then return. But first he called his servants and gave each of them a gold coin, and said, 'See what you can earn with this while I am away.' Now his own people hated him, and they sent messengers after him to say, 'We do not want this man to rule over us'.

"The nobleman received the kingdom and returned; and he sent for the servants to whom he had given the money to see what profit they had made. The first servant came to him and said, 'Your pound, sir, has made ten more.' And he replied, 'Well done! You are a good servant. You have proved yourself trustworthy over a small amount, and you will be put in charge of ten cities.' The second servant came, and he said, 'Your pound, sir, has made five more.' And he was given charge of five cities. The third servant came, and he said, 'Sir, here is your pound. I have kept it put away in a handkerchief. I was afraid of you because you are a hard man. You draw out what you never put in, and you reap what you haven't sown.' He said to him, 'You worthless servant! I will judge you with your own words: you knew I was a hard man, did you? Then why didn't you put my money in the bank? Then I would have received it back with interest when I returned!' Turning to his attendants he said, 'Take the coin from him and give it to the man who has ten.' 'But sir,' they said, 'he already has ten coins!'

'I tell you,' he replied, 'to everyone who has, more shall be given; but from the man who has nothing shall be taken even the little he thinks he has. And as for these enemies who did not want me for their king, bring them here and slay them before me.' "

J 11:1

(J 12:3

p. 83)

A man who lived in Bethany fell sick. He was Mary's brother, Lazarus. This was Mary who (later) poured perfumed oil over Jesus' feet and wiped them with her hair. They and their sister, Martha, lived together in Bethany. The two sisters sent a message to Jesus: "Lord, your dear friend is very ill." When Jesus heard this he said, "Lazarus is not going to die of this illness. This has happened to bring glory to God, and to bring glory to his Son." Now Jesus loved Martha and her sister and Lazarus dearly, yet it was two whole days that he waited before saying to his disciples,

(J 10:31)

p. 57)

"Let's go back to Jerusalem." "Rabbi," they said, "only a short time ago the Jews there wanted to stone you – and you want to go back there?" Jesus said, "There are twelve hours of daylight. Anyone can walk about in daylight without stumbling because he sees the light of this world. But if he walks at night he stumbles because there's no light for him." Then he said, "Our friend, Lazarus, has fallen asleep; but I am going to Bethany to wake him." The disciples said, "But if he's sleeping, Lord, that means he'll be getting better." They thought that Jesus was talking about ordinary sleep; but Jesus meant that Lazarus had died. So he said plainly to them, "Lazarus is dead. But for your sake I am glad that I wasn't with him – for the good of your faith. Let's go to him." Thomas, the one called 'the Twin,' said "Let's all go with the Rabbi; we can but die with him . . ."

J 11:17

By the time he arrived Jesus found that Lazarus had been buried for four days. Many Jews had come to comfort the sisters after their brother's death, Bethany being only two miles from Jerusalem. When Martha heard that Jesus was coming she went out to meet him, but Mary stayed at home. "If only you had been here, Lord," Martha said, "my brother wouldn't have died. Even now, I know that God will give you whatever you ask." Jesus said to her, "Your brother will rise again." "I know he'll rise again at the resurrection on the Last Day," she said. Jesus said, "But I am the resurrection and the life. If a man puts his faith in me, even if he dies, he will come to life again; and no one who is alive and has faith shall ever die. Do you believe this?" "Yes, Lord; I do," said Martha. "I now believe that you are the Messiah, the son of God, who was to come into the world." And she went back to the house to Mary, and said to her softly, "The Rabbi's here. He's calling for you." Mary jumped up and hurried to meet Jesus; and the Jews who were in the house to comfort Mary saw her leave the house, and they followed her, thinking that she was going to the tomb to weep there. When Mary reached the place where Jesus was, she flung herself at his feet. "Oh sir," she said. "If only you had been here, my brother would not have died." When Jesus saw her tears, and her companions weeping too, it wrung his heart. "Where have you buried him?" he asked. "Come, and we will show you, Lord," they said. Jesus wept. And the Jews said, "You can see how dearly he must have loved him." But some said, "He opened the blind man's eyes. Couldn't he have done something to keep Lazarus from dying?"

J 11:38 Jesus sighed heavily. Then he went over to the tomb. It was a cave with a stone placed against it. Jesus said, "Take away the stone." But Martha said, "Sir, by now there will be a stench – he has been dead four days . . ." Jesus said, "Didn't I tell you – if you have faith, you will see the glory of God?" So they removed the stone.

Jesus lifted up his eyes and said, "Father, I thank you. You have heard me. I know that you always hear me, but I speak for the sake of the people here, so that they may believe that you sent me."

J 11:43 Then he called out in a ringing voice, "Lazarus! Come out!"

The dead man came out. His hands and feet were swathed in linen bands and his face was wrapped in cloth. Jesus said, "Untie him, and let him walk."

Many of the Jews who had come to visit Mary saw what Jesus did – and believed in him. But others of them went back to tell the Pharisees what had happened, and what Jesus had done.

M 26:3 The chief priests immediately called a Council meeting. "What action are we to take?" they said. "This man is performing many miracles. If we let him go on like this, soon everyone will believe in him, and then the Romans will take action – they'll destroy the Temple – and the whole nation."

But Caiaphas, the High Priest, said, "You know nothing. Don't you realise that it's better to have one man die – for the people – than to let the whole nation be destroyed?" Caiaphas did not say this of his own accord. Being High Priest in office that year (a 'holy one of the Lord') he was actually prophesying that Jesus was about to die for the nation – and not only for the nation, but also to bring together the scattered children of God.

J 11:47
Mk 14:1 So, from that day onwards, they laid plans to arrest Jesus secretly and put him to death. "We must not do it during the Feast," they said, "or the people will riot." But Jesus no longer let

himself be seen in public in Judea; he went into the countryside near the desert, to a town called Ephraim, where he stayed with his disciples.

M 26:6
Mk 14:3
J 12:1

Six days before the Passover, Jesus went to Bethany, where Lazarus lived – the man he had raised from the dead. Here a dinner was given in his honour at the house of Simon, the leper. Martha served at this dinner and Lazarus sat among the guests with Jesus.

Then Mary brought a pound of very costly perfumed oil in a small phial. It was spikenard; and she broke open the phial and anointed Jesus' feet, and wiped them with her hair, until the whole house was filled with the fragrance. The son of Simon Iscariot, Judas, the one who was to betray Jesus, thought this a wicked extravagance. That perfume could have been sold for thirty pounds," he said, "and the money given to the poor." He said this, not because he cared deeply about the poor, but because he was mean. Also he was in charge of the common purse, and would sometimes even help himself to money from it. But Jesus said, "Leave her alone. This is a beautiful thing she has done for me. She has anointed me for my burial – a little beforehand, that's all. The poor will always be with you, and you will be able to help them at any time you wish; but I will not always be with you. I tell you, wherever in the world this gospel is proclaimed, she will be remembered for what she has done."

J 12:9

Many Jews heard that Jesus was there and they came to the house, not only to see Jesus, but also to have a good look at Lazarus, who had been raised from the dead. Then the chief priests decided to do away with Lazarus too, for, because of him, many Jews were leaving their leaders and putting their faith in Jesus.

J 11:55

With the approach of the Passover Festival many people were coming into Jerusalem from the surrounding countryside to go through the purification ceremonies before the Feast. They looked for Jesus. In the Temple they were asking each other, "What do you think? Do you think that perhaps he won't come to the Feast?" The chief priests and the Pharisees had given orders that anyone who knew of Jesus' whereabouts must inform the Council, so that they could arrest him.

M 21:1
Mk 11:1
L 19:28

The day after the dinner at Simon the leper's house, Jesus sent two of his disciples into Bethphage, a little village near Bethany, on the Mount of Olives. "As you go into the village," he told them,

Mk 11:3   "you'll see a donkey tethered, and her colt with her, which has never been ridden. Untie them and bring them to me. If anyone asks you what you're doing, say, 'The master needs them' – and they will let you take them at once."

The two disciples set off on their errand and found everything just as Jesus had said. As they were untying the colt, the owners who were standing there, asked them what they were doing. They answered as Jesus had told them, and they were allowed to take the beasts. They brought them to Jesus, and threw their coats on the colt's back for Jesus to mount; and they carpeted the road with

J 12:16   their coats as he went on his way. Others spread brushwood which
Zech 9:9   they had gathered in the fields. The disciples did not understand this at the time, but after Jesus had been raised to glory they remembered the Scripture's prophecy, and that they had played a part in fulfilling it. « Rejoice indeed, O maiden Zion! Shout! Shout aloud, dear Jerusalem! Behold! Thy King cometh unto thee, triumphant and victorious, riding humbly upon an ass, and upon a colt, the foal of an ass. »

L 19:37   And now, as he came down the road from the Mount of Olives, the whole company of his disciples began to sing aloud for joy. They sang praises to God for all the things they had seen: "Blessings on him who comes as King in the name of the Lord! Peace in heaven! Glory in highest heaven!"

L 19:39   Some of the Pharisees who were in the crowd said to him, "Master, tell your disciples to be quiet." Jesus answered, "I tell you, if my disciples keep quiet, the very stones will shout!"

J 12:17   The crowd that had been with Jesus when he called Lazarus out of the grave, and raised him from death, had told what they had seen and heard; and when people heard of this great miracle, they all joined the crowd on the road. And the Pharisees said to each other, "You see? We're getting nowhere. The whole world's following him!"

J 12:12   The crowds which had arrived in Jerusalem had heard that Jesus was on his way into the city, and they gathered branches of palm and went out to meet him, shouting hosannas.

L 19:41   But, as he approached the city, Jesus wept over it. He said, "If only you knew, even on this your great day, the way that leads to peace! But no; you cannot see it. For a time is coming when your enemies will lay seige against you. You will be encircled and hemmed in at every point; and they will utterly destroy you and the people within your walls. Not one stone will be left standing on another – all because you did not know your God at the time when He came to save you."

M 21:10   When Jesus entered Jerusalem the whole city was thrown into uproar. "Who is he?" the people asked. The crowd answered. "This is the prophet Jesus, from Nazareth, in Galilee."

Mk 11:11   He rode into the city and went into the Temple. And by the time he had looked at everything round and about, it was evening; and he went with his disciples to Bethany.

M 21:23   When Jesus returned to the Temple the next day, he was
Mk 11:27   teaching the people and preaching the Good News when chief
L 20:1   priests and lawyers and elders came up and accosted him. "Tell us," they demanded, "by what authority you are acting in this way. Who gave you the right?"

Jesus said, "I, too, will ask one question. Answer me this: Did John's right to baptise come from God, or from men?" This put them in a quandary. "If we say, 'From God,' he will say, 'Then why did you not believe John?' But if we say, 'From men,' the whole crowd will stone us, for they are convinced that John was a prophet." So they answered, "We can't tell where it came from." And Jesus said to them, "Then neither will I tell you by whose authority I do these things.

M 21:28   "But what do you think about this? A man had two sons. He went to the first and said, 'Son, go and work in the vineyard today.' 'I will, sir' the lad replied. But he didn't go. The man went to his second son and said the same. The second son said, 'No. I don't want to work in the vineyard today.' But later he changed his mind, and he did go into the vineyard. Now which of these two sons did the will of his father?" "The second son," they replied. "And I tell you this," Jesus said, "tax-gatherers and prostitutes will get into the Kingdom of God before you do; for when John came to show you the right way to live, you didn't believe him; but tax-gatherers and prostitutes did. And, even when you had seen that, you didn't later change your minds and believe him.

M 21:33   "Listen to another parable: A certain landowner planted a
Mk 12:1   vineyard. He put a fence round it, dug a winepress inside it, and
L 20:9   built a watch tower. Then he let it out to wine-growers and went abroad. As grape-harvest approached, he sent his servants to the tenants to collect the produce due to him. But they took his servants and they thrashed one, murdered another and stoned the third. Again the man sent servants, more this time, and the tenants treated them in the same way. Last of all he sent his own dear son. 'They will respect my son,' he said. But when the tenants saw the son, they said to each other, 'This is the heir. Come on, let's kill him, and the vineyard will be ours.' They seized him and threw

him out of the vineyard, and they killed him. Now, when the owner of the vineyard comes, how do you think he's going to deal with those tenants?" "He will certainly kill those evil men," they answered; "and leave the vineyard to tenants who will give him his rightful share when it is due."

M 21:42
Mk 12:10
L 20:17
Psa. 118:22

Jesus said to them, "Have you never read the Scripture: 'The stone which the builders rejected has become the cornerstone!. This is the Lord's doing, and it is wonderful in our eyes'. And so I tell you, the Kingdom of God will be taken away from you and given to a nation that will yield the proper fruits. Any man who falls on this cornerstone is dashed to pieces; and if it falls on a man, it will crush him to dust."

L 22:2

The lawyers and the chief priests wanted to lay hands on him there and then, for they saw that this parable was aimed at them; but they were afraid of the people, who looked on Jesus as a prophet. So they bided their time.

M 22:1
(L 14:15
p. 75–
another
version for
another
occasion)

Then Jesus told the people another parable: "The Kingdom of Heaven is like this," he said: "There was once a king who prepared a feast for his son's wedding. But when he sent his servants to summon the guests he had invited, they would not come. So he sent other servants with the message: 'See now, I have prepared this feast for you; I have had my bullocks and my prize beasts slaughtered; everything is ready – come to the wedding feast!' But they took no notice, and merely went about their business. One went off to his farm, another to his warehouse, while the rest seized his servants, beat them and killed them. The king was very angry indeed; and he sent his troops to kill those murderers and burn down their city. Then he said to the servants, 'The wedding feast is ready, but the guests I invited do not deserve the honour. Go out into the thoroughfares and invite anyone you can find to the wedding.' So the servants went out into the streets and gathered all the people they could find, good and bad alike. And the wedding hall was filled with guests.

"The king came in to see the people at table, and he noticed that one man was not wearing his wedding clothes. 'My friend,' said the king, 'how do you come to be here without your wedding clothes?' But the man had nothing to say. Then the king told his servants, 'Tie him up hand and foot, and throw him outside in the dark, the place of wailing and grinding of teeth.' For, though many are invited, few are chosen."

M 21:14

The blind and the crippled came to him in the Temple and he healed them. The chief priests and doctors of the Law saw the wonderful things he did, and heard the children in the Temple shouting, "Hosanna to the Son of David!" And they asked him indignantly, "Do you hear what they are saying?" Jesus answered, "I do indeed. But have you never read the text: 'Out of the mouths of babes and sucklings hast thou perfected praise'?" Then he left them, and went out of the city to Bethany, where he spent the night.

M 22:15
Mk 12:13
L 20:20

The chief priests and doctors of the Law were just waiting for a chance to trap Jesus with crafty questions. They sent some of their disciples and some of Herod's party to him, in the guise of honest men, hoping that some word of his would give them a pretext for handing him over to the authority and power of the Governor. "Master," they said, "we know that you teach the truth about the way of God, and you're no respecter of persons. Tell us, is it lawful, or not, to pay tribute to Caesar? Should we pay or not?" Jesus realised how cunning the question was. He said, "Bring me a silver coin, and let me look at it." They handed him a coin, and he said. "Whose head is this, whose inscription?" "Caesar's," they said. "Then," said Jesus, "pay to Caesar what belongs to him, and pay to God what belongs to God." His reply left them confounded, and they could find nothing to say.

G

Then some Sadduces came forward. They are the people who hold that there is no life after death. "Master," they said, "Moses laid it down for us that if a man should die leaving his wife childless, then his brother should marry her and raise children for the family. Well, once there were seven brothers. The first took a wife, but he died without having any children. Then the next brother married the widow, and he died before she had any children. The same thing happened to the third brother, and then to all the rest: all seven brothers married the woman and died without having any children. Last of all the woman died. Now, if all the dead are raised to life on the day of resurrection, whose wife will she be? All seven of them married her."

Jesus answered, "You are mistaken because you know neither the Scriptures nor the power of God. The men and women of this world marry; but those who have been judged worthy of a place in the other world, and of resurrection from the dead – they do not marry because they are not subject to death any longer. They are like angels. They are the sons of God because they share in the resurrection.

Ex. 3:1-6

"But, about the resurrection of the dead, you are told, in Moses' account of the burning bush, that the dead will be raised to life: God said to him « I am the God of Abraham, the God of Isaac, and the God of Jacob. » Now he is not God of the dead; he is God

of the living – for all are alive to him." The people heard his words
and they were astonished at his teaching.

M 22:34   Then one of the lawyers who had been listening to these
Mk 12:28   discussions and had seen how well Jesus had answered, came
(L 10:25-39) forward and asked him, "Which commandment is the most
important of all?" Jesus answered, "The first commandment is:
'Hear, O Israel! The Lord your God is the only Lord. Love the Lord
your God with all your heart, with all your soul, with all your mind
and with all your strength.' The second is this: 'Love your
neighbour as yourself.' There is no other commandment greater
Mk 12:32   than these." The lawyer said to him, "Well said, Master! You are
right in saying that there is one God, and beside him there is no
other. And to love him with all your understanding and all your
strength, and to love your neighbour as yourself – that is far more
than any burnt offerings or sacrifices." When Jesus saw how wisely
he spoke, he said to him, "You are not far from the Kingdom of
God."

M 22:41   A group of Pharisees had assembled nearby; and Jesus turned
Mk 12:35   to them and asked, "What is your opinion about the Messiah?
L 20:41   Whose son is he?" They replied, "He is the Son of David." "Why,
then," Jesus said, "did the Spirit inspire David to call him 'Lord'?
For David said, 'The Lord said unto my Lord « Sit thou at my right
hand till I make thine enemies thy footstool »' If David calls him
'Lord,' how then can he be David's son?" No man could think of a
(L 20:40)   word to say in reply; and from that day on, no one ventured to ask
him any further questions.

M 23:1   Jesus then spoke to the people and the disciples. "The teachers
Mk 12:38   of the Law and the Pharisees," he said, "sit in the chair of Moses.
L 20:45   Therefore you must obey them. Pay careful attention to their
L 11:46   words. Do not, however, imitate their actions, because they do not
practice what they preach. They make up very heavy burdens and
tie them on men's backs; but they themselves will not lift a finger
M 23:5   to help them carry those loads. Everything is done for show. See!
How large are those phylacteries of verses from the Scriptures they
wear on their foreheads! – and how deep the fringes on their
L 11:43   cloaks! They love to sit in places of honour at feasts, and in the
reserved seats in the synagogues; and they like to be greeted very
respectfully in the streets, and to be called 'Rabbi.'

M 23:8   "But you must call no one 'Teacher,' for you have one Teacher –
Christ. And you are all brothers. Do not call any man on earth,
'Father,' for you have one Father, and he is in Heaven. Nor should
you call anyone 'Master,' because your one and only Master is the
Messiah. The greatest among you must be your servant; for

M 23:12   whoever exalts himself will be humbled; and whoever humbles himself will be exalted.

L 11:52   "Alas for you, lawyers and Pharisees! Hypocrites! You shut the door of the Kingdom of Heaven in men's faces; you yourselves will not go in, and you stop others who are trying to enter.

M 23:14
Mk 12:40
L 20:47   "Alas for you, lawyers and Pharisees! Hypocrites! You rob widows of their homes, and then make a show of saying long prayers! Because of this your punishment will be all the worse.

"Alas for you, lawyers and Pharisees! Hypocrites! You sail the seas and cross whole countries to win one convert. And when you have succeeded, you make him twice as fit for hell as you are!

"Alas for you, blind guides! You say: 'If a man swears by the

M23:16   Sanctuary he's not bound by his oath; but if he swears by the gold in the Sanctuary, he is bound'! You are blind and stupid! Which is more important – the gold? – or the Sanctuary which makes it

See also
M 5:34
p. 24   holy? To swear by the altar, then, is to swear by the altar and whatever lies upon it; to swear by the Sanctuary is to swear by the Sanctuary and by him who dwells there; and to swear by heaven is to swear both by the throne of God and by Him who sits upon it.

M 23:23
L 11:42   "Alas for you, lawyers and Pharisees! Hypocrites! You carefully give to God a tithe even of your seasoning herbs – mint, dill and cumin – but you neglect the much weightier teachings of the Law – justice, mercy and honesty! These you should practice first – but without forgetting the others. Blind guides! You strain a midge out of your drink, but you'll swallow a camel!

M 23:25
L 11:39
(See also
p. 72)   "Alas for you, lawyers and Pharisees! Hypocrites! You clean the outside of your cup and dish, while the inside is full of things you have got through violence and selfishness! Blind Pharisees! Clean the inside of your cup first, then the outside will be clean too.

"Alas for you, lawyers and Pharisees! Hypocrites! You are like whitewashed tombs: they look good on the outside, but inside they are full of dead men's bones and all kinds of filth. Just so with you; from the outside you look like honest men, but inside you are full of hypocrisy and iniquity.

L 11:47   "Alas for you, lawyers and Pharisees! Hypocrites! You build fine tombs for the prophets, and you decorate the monuments of the saints; and you say, 'If we had lived in those times of our ancestors, we would not have done what they did and murdered the prophets.' In saying this, you are actually admitting that you are the sons of those men who killed the Prophets. Go on then – finish off what your fathers began!

M 23:33   "You serpents! Brood of vipers! How can you escape being condemned to hell? This is why the wisdom of God said: « I will send you prophets, wise men, and teachers. Some of them you will kill, and crucify; others you will flog in your synagogues and hound from city to city » As a result, upon you will fall the punishment for the shedding of all this innocent blood – from innocent Abel to Zechariah, Barachiah's son, whom you murdered between the Sanctuary and the altar. Believe me, this generation will bear the guilt of it all.

M 23:37
L 13:34

"O Jerusalem City that murders the prophets and stones the messengers God has sent to you! How often have I longed to gather all your children in my arms, as a hen gathers her brood under her wings! But you would not let me. And now – look! There is your Temple, forsaken by God. And I tell you that from now on, you will never see me again until the time when you say, 'Blessings on him who comes in the name of the Lord!' "

Mk 12:41
L 21:1

Jesus was sitting near the Temple treasury, and he was watching people as they dropped their money into one of the coffers. Many rich people were giving large sums. Presently a poor woman came along and dropped in two small copper coins – worth about a penny. He called his disciples to him, and he said, "I tell you, this poor widow has put more money into the offering box than all the others. For those others who have given have riches to spare; but she, with less than enough, has given everything she had. She has put in the money she needs to live on."

M 24:1
Mk 13:1
L 21:5

As they were leaving the Temple one of the disciples exclaimed, "Just look at it, Master! What huge stones! What magnificent buildings they are!" And Jesus said to him, "Yes. Take a good, long look at them while you can. I tell you, not one of these stones will be left in its place. Every last one will be thrown down."

M 24:3
Mk 13:3
L 17:22
L 21:7

When Jesus was sitting down, on the Mount of Olives, looking at the Temple, Peter, James, John and Andrew spoke to him privately. "Tell us when all this will happen," they said. "How will we know when you are coming, and the end of the age is near?" Jesus said, "The time will come when you will long to see one of the days of the Son of Man; but you will not see it. But you must watch out. Don't be misled. For many false prophets will appear. They will come in my name, and they will say, 'I am the Messiah!' and 'The day is upon us!' 'The time has come!' Do not follow them. And when you hear of wars and revolutions, near at hand and far off, don't be afraid. These things must happen first, but they do not mean that the end is near. Nation will make war against nation, kingdom against kingdom. There will be earthquakes and famines and plagues in many places; and there will be awful portents and signs in the heavens. All these things will be like the first birth-pangs of the sorrow to come.

M 24:23
Mk 13:21
L 17:23

"And I tell you those impostors will come, claiming to be the Messiah, or prophets; and they will produce great signs and wonders – enough to mislead God's chosen, if such a thing were possible. But see – I have forewarned you. If they say to you, 'Look! He's out there in the wilderness!' – don't go there; never run after them. And if they say, 'Look! He's in hiding here!' – don't believe it. As the lightning flashes across the sky from east to west and lights it up from one side to the other, so it will be with the Son of Man on his Day. But first he must endure much suffering and be rejected by the people of this day.

M 24:9
(M 10:17)
Mk 13:9
L 21:12
L 12:11

"But before all this happens you will be arrested and persecuted. You will be brought before the synagogues, and put in prison; and you will be dragged before kings and rulers for my sake. But this will be your chance to tell the Good News. Make up your minds in advance not to cudgel your brains about what you are going to say in your defence; for I will give you such words of wisdom that none of your enemies will be able to refute or deny what you say. The words you speak will not be yours – they will come from the Holy Spirit.

M 10:21
Mk 13:12
L 21:16

"You will be betrayed—even by your own brothers, your relatives and friends; some of you will be put to death, and you will be hated by all for your allegiance to me. But not a hair of your heads will be lost. Hold firm and steadfast and you will win your souls. Many will lose faith. They will betray one another, and hate each other. And as evil spreads, the love of the many will grow cold.

M 24:15
Mk 13:14
L 21:20
L 17:31

"When you see Jerusalem besieged by armies, then you may be sure her destruction is near. You will see 'the abomination of desolation' of which Daniel spoke, standing in the Holy Place, where he has no right to stand – let the reader understand the allusion. Then those who are in Judea must take to the hills. Those who are in the city itself must leave it; and those who are out in the countryside must not come into the city. A man who is on the roof of his house, must not take the time to go back to get his belongings from inside the house. The man who is in the fields must not go back to get his coat – remember Lot's wife. And the man who seeks to save his own life will lose it; but he who is prepared to lose his life will save it and live. I tell you, on that night

M 24:40 there will be two men in one bed; one will be taken and the other left. Two women will be grinding meal together; one will be taken away, and the other left behind. Two men will be in the field; one will be taken, and the other left." When the disciples heard this, they asked, "Where, Lord?" And he said, "Where there is a dead

M 24:28 body the vultures will gather.

L 21:22 "This is the time of punishment when all that is written in the Scriptures will be fulfilled. Terrible distress will come upon this land, and God's wrath will be against this people. They will be killed by the sword, and taken prisoner to all countries. And Jerusalem will be trampled down by foreigners until the Gentiles' time is ended.

M 24:14 "First the Gospel of the Kingdom will be proclaimed throughout

Mk 13:10 the earth as a testimony to all nations; and then the end will come.

Mk 13:17 How terrible it will be in those days for women who are with child, and for mothers with little babies! Pray that it may not come in winter. For those days will bring such distress as has never been seen until now, not since the beginning of the world which God created – and never will be again. If the Lord had not cut short that time of troubles, no living thing could survive. But for the sake of his chosen people, God has cut short the time.

M 24:29 "In those days, after that great distress, the sun will be

Mk 13:24 darkened and the moon will not give her light. On earth, nations

L 21:25 will be in despair, not knowing which way to turn from the roaring of the sea and its raging tides, fainting with fear of what is coming to the earth; for the stars will come falling from the heavens, and the powers of space will be shaken from their course. Then will appear in the heavens the sign that heralds the coming of the Son of Man. All the peoples of the world will groan and lament; and they will see the Son of Man coming in the clouds of heaven in power and great glory. The great trumpet will sound, and he will send his angels to the four corners of the earth, and they will gather his chosen people from one end of the earth to the other. When these things begin to happen, stand up – and raise your heads for your salvation is near.

M 24:32 "Let the fig tree teach you a parable: as soon as the branches

Mk 13:28 turn soft and put out leaves, you know that summer is at hand; so

L 21:29 when you see these things begin to happen you will know that he is at hand, at the very door. I tell you truly, the present generation will not pass away until all this happens. Heaven and earth will pass away, but my words – never.

M 24:36 "Now, no one knows when that day, that hour, will come –

Mk 13:32   neither the angels in heaven, nor even the Son. Only the Father knows. So be always on the watch, always wide awake, for you don't know when that time will be. It will be like the man who has gone away from home. He has put the servants in charge, each with his own job to do; and he has told the door-keeper to keep watch. So watch! – for you don't know when the master will return. Evening or midnight, before dawn or at sunrise – if he comes suddenly, he mustn't find you asleep. I say this to you, and I say it to everyone: watch and pray!

M 24:37
L 17:26   "As it was in the time of Noah, so shall it be in the days of the Son of Man. Everyone went on eating and drinking, men and women were getting married, until the day came that destroyed them all. And it will be as it was in the time of Lot – everyone kept on eating and drinking, buying and selling, planting, building. On the day that Lot left Sodom, fire and sulphur rained down from heaven upon Sodom and killed them all. It will be like that on the day when the Son of Man is revealed.

L 21:34   "Keep a watch on yourselves. Don't let your minds become dulled with too much feasting and strong drink, and worldly cares, so that the great Day closes on you suddenly, like a trap. That Day will come upon all men, wherever they are, the whole world over. Keep awake hour by hour, and pray that you will have the strength to go safely through all these things which are going to happen, and to stand in the presence of the Son of Man.

M 25:1   "On that Day the Kingdom of Heaven will be like this: Ten girls took their lamps to go out to meet the bridegroom. Five of them were foolish, and five of them were wise. When the foolish girls took their lamps they didn't think to take any extra oil with them; but the wise ones took little flasks of oil with theirs.

    "The bridegroom was late, and they all began to drop off to sleep. Then, at midnight, the cry rang out: 'The bridegroom is here! Come out and meet him!' All the girls got up and trimmed their lamps. 'Oh look!' said the foolish ones. 'Our lamps are going out! Give us some of your oil.' But the wise ones said, 'No. There won't be enough for all of us. Better hurry to the shops and buy yourselves some more.' So the foolish girls went off to buy more oil, and while they were away the bridegroom arrived. Those who were ready went with him to the wedding, and the door was closed. And then the other five came back. 'Sir, sir!' they cried. 'Open the door for us.' But he said, 'I really don't know you.' Keep awake then, for you never know the day or the hour.

M 25:31   "When the Son of Man comes as King, and all the angels with him, he will sit in state on his throne, and all the people of the earth will be gathered before him. Then he will divide them into two groups, just as the shepherd separates the sheep from the goats; and he will put the sheep at his right hand and the goats at his left. Then the King will say to the people at his right hand: 'Come, you who are blessed by my Father; come and receive the Kingdom which has been prepared for you ever since the world began. For when I was hungry you fed me, and when I was thirsty you gave me a drink; when I was a stranger you took me into your home; and when naked you clothed me.' The honest people will say to him, 'When was it, Lord, that we ever saw you hungry and fed you, or thirsty and gave you a drink; a stranger and took you home, or naked and clothed you? When did we see you ill or in prison, and come to visit you?' And the King will answer, 'I tell you truly that whenever you did it for one of these my brothers, even for the least of them, you did it for me.'

M 25:41   "And then the King will turn to those at his left hand: 'Away from me, you who are under God's curse! Away to the eternal fire which has been prepared for the devil and his angels! I was hungry, but you would not feed me; thirsty, but you would not give me a drink. I was a stranger, but you would not welcome me into your homes; naked, but you never clothed me. I was ill and in prison, but you did not come to my aid.' And they will answer him, 'Lord, when did we ever see you hungry, or thirsty, or a stranger, or naked, or sick, or in prison, and would not help you?' The King will answer them, 'I tell you, indeed, that whenever you refused to help one of the least of these, you refused to help me.' These will be sent to eternal punishment; but the righteous will go to eternal life."

L 21:37   Jesus spent those days teaching in the Temple, and when evening came he would go out and spend the night on the Mount of Olives. All the people would go to the Temple early in the morning to listen to him.

M 26:14   One of the disciples, the one called Judas Iscariot, went to the
Mk 14:10   chief priests and said, "What would you give me to betray him to
L 22:3   you?" They were very pleased to hear these words, and they counted out thirty pieces of silver and gave them to him. Then Judas started looking for some means of leading them to Jesus without attracting a crowd.

J 12:20   Among those who went up to Jerusalem to worship at the Festival were some Greeks. They came to Philip, who was from Bethsaida in Galilee, and said to him, "Sir, we would like to see Jesus." So Philip went and told Andrew, and the two of them went to tell Jesus.

J 12:23 And Jesus said, "The hour has come for the Son of Man to be glorified. Truly, truly I tell you, unless a grain of wheat falls into the earth and dies, it remains – just a grain of wheat. But if it dies, then it yields a rich harvest. The man who loves himself is lost, but he who cares nothing for his life in this world will be kept safe for eternal life. If anyone serves me, he must follow me; where I am, there my servant will be. And whoever serves me will be honoured by my Father.

J 12:27 "Now, oh now, my soul is troubled. But what am I to say? – 'Father save me from this hour.'? No. It was for this that I came – to go through this hour of suffering. Father! Glorify your name!"

And a voice sounded from heaven « I have glorified my name. And I will glorify it again »

The crowd heard the voice, and some said, "It was thunder." But others said, "No. An angel spoke to him." Jesus said to them, "The voice spoke for your sake, not for mine. Now the time has come for the world to be judged. Now the prince of this world will be cast out. And when I am lifted up from the earth I shall draw all men to me." He said this to show what kind of death he would suffer.

J 12:34 The people answered, "Our Law says that the Messiah will live for ever." "What do you mean – 'the Son of Man will be lifted up'?" "What Son of Man is this?" Jesus replied, "The Light is among you still, but not for long. Go on your way while you still have light, so that the darkness may not overtake you. The man who travels in the dark doesn't know where he is going. While you have the light, then, believe in it; trust it, so that you will become people of the light."

After saying this, Jesus went away and hid himself from them. Even though he had performed all these wonderful signs before their very eyes, some of them did not believe in him. Jesus had

(J 6:44) said, "No one can come to me unless the Father who sent me
p. 48 draws him to me." And the ancient prophecies were fulfilled:
Isa. 53:1 Isaiah said, "Lord, who has believed the message we told? To
Isa. 6:9-10 whom has the Lord revealed his power?" So it was that they could not believe. Isaiah said again. "God has blinded their eyes. He has closed their minds « so that their eyes would not see, their minds would not understand, and they would not turn to me and let me heal them »." Isaiah said these words because he 'saw' Jesus' glory, and it was of him that he spoke to the people. For all that, many did believe in him, including Jewish leaders; but they did not admit it in public because of the Pharisees. They did not want to be barred from the synagogue, because the approval of

their fellow men was more important to them than the approval of God.

J 12:44 Jesus cried in a loud voice, "Whoever believes in me believes in him who sent me. Whoever sees me, sees him who sent me. I have come into the world as Light; and anyone who believes in me will never be in darkness. If anyone hears my message and does not believe it, I will not judge him. I came to save the world, not to judge it. But there is One who will judge those who reject me and refuse to accept my message: the Word I have spoken will be their judge on the Last Day. I do not speak on my own authority; but the Father who sent me has commanded me – what I am to say and how to speak. I know that his commands are eternal life. What the Father has said to me, therefore, that is what I speak."

M 26:17
Mk 14:12
L 22:7
J 13:1
It was the evening before the Passover Festival, the first day of the Feast of Unleavened Bread, and the day the lambs for the Passover Feast were killed. Jesus knew that his hour had come, and that now he had to leave this world and go to the Father. He had always loved those who were his own in the world, and he would love them to the very end.

Jesus' disciples asked him, "Where do you want us to go to prepare your Passover supper?" So Jesus sent two of his disciples out with his instructions: "Go into the city and you will see a man carrying a jar of water. Follow him to the house he enters and give this message to the owner of the house: The master says, "Where is the room reserved for me to eat the Passover meal with my disciples?" He will show you a large room upstairs, all ready set out. Prepare the Passover for us there." The disciples set off, and when they came to the city they found everything just as Jesus had told them. So they made preparations for the Passover supper.

M 26:20
Mk 14:17
L 22:14
1 Cor.11:23
In the evening he came to the house with the Twelve. He took his place at table, and the apostles with him; and he said to them, "How I have longed to eat this Passover meal with you before my death! For I tell you, never again shall I eat it until the time when it finds fulfilment in the Kingdom of my Father." Then he took a cup, and after giving thanks, he said, "Take this, all of you, and drink from it; for I tell you, from this moment I shall drink of the fruit of the vine no more until the time when I drink it new, with you, in my Father's Kingdom."

Mk 14:25

And, during supper, he took bread and, having said the blessing, he broke it and gave it to his disciples with the words: "Take this, and eat. This is my body which is given for you; do this in memory of me." And in the same way, after supper he took the

Mk 14:22

cup and he said, "This cup is poured out for many for the forgiveness of sins. It is the New Covenant, sealed by my blood. Whenever you drink it do this to remember me."

J 13:2　　Although he knew that the devil had already invaded the heart and mind of Judas Iscariot and that Judas would betray him, Jesus knew well that the Father had given him complete power — that he had come from God and he was going back to God. He got up from the table, laid aside his robe and picked up a towel which he tied round his waist. Then he poured water into a bowl and began to wash his disciples' feet. As he came to Simon Peter, Peter said, "Lord, are you going to wash my feet?" Jesus said, "You don't understand now what I'm doing, Peter, but one day you will know." But Peter said roundly, "Never, Lord! I will never let you wash my feet!" Jesus said, "Peter, if I do not wash your feet you cannot be with me." Simon Peter said to him, "Then, Lord — not only my feet. Wash my hands, and my head . . ." But Jesus said, "A man who has just bathed needs only to wash his feet. He is quite clean. And all of you are clean – except one . . ." He knew who was going to betray him.

J 13:12　　After he had washed their feet Jesus put on his robe and went back to his place at table and sat down. He said to them, "Do you understand what I have just done for you? You call me 'Rabbi' and 'Lord', and that is right, for so I am. Then if I, your Lord and Master, have washed your feet, you too ought also to wash one another's feet. I have set an example for you; you are to do as I have done for you. Remember this: a servant is not more important than his master, nor is a messenger more important than the one who sent him. And if you understand that – then happy are you if you act upon it!

J 13:18　　"I am not speaking of all of you. I know whom I have chosen –
Mk 14:18　but there is another word in the Scripture which has to come true: 'He who eats bread with me has turned against me.' I am telling you this now, before it has happened, so that when it does come true, you will believe that « I am who I am. » And I will tell you another truth: whoever receives any messenger I send, receives me; and to receive me is to receive the One who sent me."

J 13:21　　After these words Jesus was deeply troubled. "In truth I tell you,
M 26:21　one of you here at table with me is going to betray me," he said. The disciples looked at each other in dismay. Then they began asking Jesus which one of them would betray him. One after another they said, "Surely it's not me?" "It's not me, is it Lord?"

The disciple whom Jesus loved was sitting close to the Master.

J 13:24	Simon Peter nodded to him and said quietly, "Ask him who it is." And the disciple close to Jesus leaned towards him and said,
Mk 14:20	"Lord, who is it?" Jesus replied, "It is the man to whom I will give this piece of bread when I have dipped it in the dish. The Son of
L 22:21	Man is going the way appointed for him in the Scriptures; but alas for that man by whom he is betrayed! It would be better for him if he had never been born." Then Judas, the son of Simon Iscariot, spoke. "Rabbi, you mean me?" Jesus replied, "The words are yours." Then, after dipping it in the dish, he gave the piece of bread to Judas; and as Judas received the bread, Satan went into him. Jesus said to him, "Whatever you have to do, do it quickly." None of the others sitting at table understood these words. As Judas was in charge of the money-bag, they thought that Jesus wanted him to buy something for the Passover Feast or, perhaps, to give some money to the poor. Judas then, having received the bread, went out into the night.
L 22:24	Then an argument broke out among the apostles about who among them should be counted as the greatest. But Jesus said to them, "Remember what I have said to you: in this world kings lord it over their subjects, and those in authority are called their country's 'benefactors.' This is not so with you. No, the highest among you must bear himself as if he were the youngest; the chief among you must be like a servant. Who do you think is greater – the man who sits at table, or the one who waits on him? Of course you will say, the one who sits down. But here am I among you as a servant.
L 22:28	"It is you who have stood by me through all my trials. And now,
L 12:32	just as the Father has given Kingship to me, so do I give you the right to eat and drink at my table in the Kingdom. And you shall sit on thrones as judges of the twelve tribes of Israel.
J 13:31	"Now the Son of Man is glorified, and in him, God is glorified. If God is glorified in him, God will also glorify him in himself."
M 26:30	After singing the Passover hymn, they went to the Mount of
Mk 14:26	Olives.
J 13: 33	Jesus said to them, "My children, I shall be with you only a little while longer. Then you will look for me and, as I told the Jews, I tell you now – where I am going you cannot come. I give you a new commandment: it is to love one another. As I have loved you, you are to love one another. If there is this love among you, then all will know that you are my disciples." Simon Peter said to him, "Lord, where are you going?" Jesus replied, "Where I am going you cannot follow me now. But one day you will." Then he said, "Simon, Simon,
L 22:31	take care! Satan has claimed the right to sift you all like wheat.

Zech. 13:7
M 26:31

Tonight all of you will fall from your faith; for it stands written: « I will strike the shepherd down, and the sheep will be scattered. » But after I am raised to life, I will go ahead of you to Galilee."

J 13:37
M 26:33
Mk 14:29
L 22:32

Peter said, "Lord, why can't I follow you now? I am ready to die for you. Even if all the rest were to desert you, I never will." Jesus said, "Peter, I tell you, before cock-crow you will have disowned me three times. But I have prayed for you that your faith may not fail; and when you have come to yourself, you must give strength to your brothers." "Lord," he replied, "I am ready to go with you to prison, and to die with you." And they all said the same.

L 22:35

Isa. 53:12

J 14:1

He said to them, "When I sent you out without purse or pack or shoes, were you in need of anything?" "No, " they said. "Nothing." "Well now," he said, "he who has a purse must take it – and a pack. And whoever has no sword had better sell his shirt and buy one. For I tell you, the words in Scripture: 'He was classed among criminals' have to come true about me. Indeed, all that is written about me is coming true. "Look, Lord," the disciples said. "Here are two swords!" "Enough! Enough!" he said. "Don't be afraid. You believe in God – believe also in me. There is more than enough room in my Father's house – room for you all. If it weren't so, I would have told you. And after I have gone ahead to prepare a place for you, I shall come back and bring you there myself, so that you will be there with me, and – you know the way I am going there . . ." Thomas said, "Lord, we don't even understand where you are going, so how can we know the way?" Jesus said to him, "I am the Way; and I am the Truth; and I am the Life. No one can reach the Father except through me.

"Now that you know me you will know my Father too. From now on you do know him. You have seen him." Philip said, "Lord, just show us the Father – that's all we need." Jesus replied, "Philip, I have been with you all this time – and yet you still don't know me? Whoever has seen me has seen the Father. So why do you say, 'Show us the Father.'? Don't you believe, Philip, that I am in the Father and the Father is in me?"

He turned to the other disciples. "I am not the source of the words I speak to you; it is the Father, who lives in me, doing his own will. You can believe me when I say that I am in the Father and the Father is in me – or you can accept the evidence of the deeds themselves; and I tell you truly that whoever has faith in me can do what I am doing. In fact, he will do even greater deeds – because I am going to the Father. Anything you ask in my name I will do, so that the Father's glory will be shown through the Son. If you ask anything in my name I will do it.

"If you love me you will keep my commandments. And I will ask the Father, and he will give you another, to be your helper and comforter, who will be with you for ever – the Spirit of Truth. The world can't receive him, or even know him, because it can't see him. But you know him. He is living with you, and one day will be in you.

"I am not going to leave you all alone – bereft and forlorn. I am going to come back to you. In only a little while now the world will see me no more. But you will. You will see me. And when that day comes you will know that I am in my Father and my Father in me. And because I will have overcome death and I am alive, you too will live – you in me, and I in you.

"The man who has heard and understood my commands, and obeys them, he it is who loves me. And he who loves me will be loved by my Father; and I will love him too, and appear in him." Judas (Thaddaeus), James' son, said, "Lord, how can it be that you will reveal yourself to us and not to the world?" Jesus answered, "Whoever loves me will obey my message. My Father will love him, and my Father and I will come to him and abide with him. But whoever doesn't love me, doesn't hear my words – the Father's words – the Father who sent me here.

"I have told you all this while I can, while I am still here with you, but the helper, the Comforter – the Holy Spirit whom the Father will send in my name – he will teach you everything, and will make you remember and understand all the things I have told you.

"My parting gift to you is peace – my own peace – such as the world cannot give you. Don't let your heart be troubled, don't let it be afraid. You have heard me say that I am going away – and that I am coming back to you. If you love me you'll be glad that I am going to the Father, because the Father is greater than I am. And I have told you this now, before it happens, so that when it comes to pass, you will have faith. I shall not be able to talk to you much longer, for the prince of this world is coming. He has no power over me but, so that the world may know that I love the Father, I carry out to the letter every command he gives me. So it's time to get up, and go.

J 15:1 "Think of it like this: I am the true vine, and my Father is the gardener. The gardener tends the vine; he cuts out all the branches which don't bear fruit. The ones that do bear fruit he prunes, to keep them healthy and to grow more fruit. You have already been made clean and healthy; you have been cleansed by the word I have spoken to you. As long as you can stay part of me, I am part of you. If you do not stay attached to me, you can't bear fruit – any more than a branch can bear fruit unless it remains attached to the vine . . .

"You see, I am the vine – and you are the branches. Whoever remains a part of me, I am a part of him, and he will bear a lot of fruit. But, apart from me – you can do nothing. Whoever fails to remain a part of me is discarded – like a withered branch. Withered branches are heaped together and burnt on the bonfire. But if you live as part of me, and my words live in you, then, ask what you will, you shall have it. This is my Father's glory – that you bear wonderful fruit. That is the way to be my disciples.

"As the Father has loved me, so I have loved you. Live in my love. If you carry out my commands you will live in my love – just as I have carried out the Father's commands, and I live in his love.

"I have told you this so that my joy can come to you, and so that you may be completely filled with that joy. This is my command: love one another as I have loved you. There is no greater love than this – that a man should lay down his life for his friends. And you are my friends if you follow my commands. You are no longer servants; servants do not know what their master's business is. You are friends because I have told you everything I heard from my Father. You didn't choose me – I chose you. And I've trained and ordained you to go and bear fruit – and fruit that will last; so that the Father will give you whatever you ask him in my name. This is my commandment to you: Love one another.

"If the world hates you, remember that it hated me first. If you belonged to this world, then the world would love you as its own. But it's because you don't belong to this world, because I have chosen you out of it, that the world hates you. Do you remember what I said, 'A servant is not greater than his master'? Just as they have persecuted me, they will persecute you; and they will follow your teaching as little as they have followed mine. They'll do all this to you because you belong to me, and they don't know the One who sent me. If I hadn't come – if I hadn't spoken to them – they would not be guilty of any sin. As it is they have no excuse for their sin. Whoever hates me is hating my Father. They would not have been guilty if I had not come, and if I hadn't done all these works among them such as no man ever did before. As it is, they have seen these works, and they hate both me and my Father. But this text in their own Law has come true: 'They hated me for no reason'.

Psalms
35:19
69:4

"But when the Comforter has come – the spirit of Truth who comes from the Father he will tell you all about me. And you will be able to tell everyone about me because you have been with me from the very beginning.

J 16:1   "And I have told you all this so that you may keep steady in your faith; because they will ban you from the synagogue. Indeed the time will come when anyone who kills you will think he is doing a service to God. They will do all these things, you see, because they know neither the Father nor me. And I have told you all this so that when the time comes, and these things happen, you will be able to remember my words to you.

"I didn't tell you these things in the beginning because then – I was with you. But now I am going away to him who sent me. None of you are asking, 'Where are you going?' And because I've told you, your hearts are heavy with sorrow. But listen, I am telling you truly – it's better for you that I go away. If I don't go, the Helper will not come to you. But if I do go – then I will send him to you. And when he comes he will prove their error to the people of the world. He will show them what is wrong, and what is right, and what God's judgment is. He will convict them of their wrong in their refusal to believe in me. He will convince them that right is on my side, by showing that I go to the Father, when you see me no more; and he will convince them of divine judgment by showing them that the prince of this world already stands condemned.

J 16:12   "I could tell you so much more – but you can't bear any more now. But when the Comforter comes he will guide you into all Truth. And he won't be speaking on his own authority, he will be telling you what he hears; and he will tell you about things to come. He will glorify me because everything he makes known to you he will have received from me. All that the Father has is mine – that is why I say to you that whatever he reveals to you he will have received from me.

"In a little while you will see me no more; and then, a little while later, you will see me again."

Some of his disciples said to each other, "What can he mean? What does he mean: 'In a little while'? – and then he says 'It is because I am going to the Father' – we can't understand this at all." Jesus knew that they wanted to ask questions; he said to them, "Are you discussing what I said? – 'a little while and you will not see me; and again a little while and you will see me.' Is that what you were wondering about? I tell you truly, you will weep and lament – but the world will rejoice. But though you will be sad, your sadness will be turned into joy. It is like a woman who is in labour: she is in pain because her hour has come; but when the baby is born, she forgets all about the pain because she is so happy that her baby is born into the world. It will be like that for you. You are sad now, but when I see you again your hearts will be filled with such gladness – the kind of gladness that no one can ever take away from you.

"When that day comes you will need to ask nothing from me. I tell you truly that if you ask the Father for anything in my name, he will give it to you. Until now you haven't asked for anything in my name. Ask! – and you will receive – that your happiness may be complete.

"I have been telling you these things in parables. But the time is coming when I will no longer need to tell you in parables, but will tell you of the Father in plain words. When that day comes, you will ask him in my name. I am not saying that I will pray to the Father for you, for the Father loves you himself – because you have loved me and believed that I came from him. Just so, I did come from my Father into the world; and now I am leaving the world to go to my Father."

His disciples said, "Well, this is plain enough speaking. No parables now. Now we know that you know everything – no more questions needed. This makes us certain that you have come from God."

Jesus answered them, "Do you now believe? Ah! I tell you that the hour is coming – indeed it is here already – when you will all be scattered, each to his own home, and I will be left alone. And yet – I am never alone because the Father is always with me. I have told you these things so that you will find peace through me. In this world you will find trouble. But hold on bravely! I have won! I have overcome the world!"

J 17:1 After speaking these words Jesus looked up into heaven and said, "Father, the hour has come. Glorify your Son so that your Son may glorify you. For you have made him sovereign over all men so that he may give eternal life to as many as you have given to him. And eternal life is to know you, the true and only God, and to know Jesus, the Christ, whom you have sent. I have given you glory on earth, and I have finished the work you gave me to do. And now, Father, glorify me in your own presence with the glory I had with you before the world was made.

"I have made your name known to the men that you gave me out of this world. They were yours, and you gave them to me; and they have obeyed your word. And now they know that all these gifts have come to me from you; for I gave them your message, and they received it. They know that truly I have come from you, and they believe that it was you who sent me. I pray for them. I am not praying for the world, but for the ones that you have given to me, because they belong to you. All that are mine are yours, and all of yours are mine; and my glory has shone through them.

J 17:11   "And now I am coming to you, and I am to be no longer in the world. But they are in the world. O Holy Father! Keep them safe, those you have given me, by the power of your name, so that they may be one as we are one. While I was with them I kept them safe by the power of your name – the name you gave me. And not one of them was lost – except the one who had to be lost, in fulfilment of the Scripture. And now I am coming to you; but while I am still in the world I am saying these words so that they may have my joy in their hearts in all its fullness.

"I gave them your message and the world hated them because they do not belong to this world any more than I do. I do not ask you to take them out of the world, but to keep them from the evil one. They are strangers in the world as I am. Make them your own by means of your word, which is Truth. I have sent them into the world just as you sent me into the world; and for their sake I give myself to you, so that they may truly belong to you.

"And I do not pray only for them, but also for those who come to believe in me because of their words. Dear Father, I pray that they all may be one; and that just as you are in me, Father, and I in you, they also may be in us. Let them be one in us, so that the world may believe that you sent me. The glory you gave me I have given to them, so that they could be one just as you and I are one – I in them, and you in me, so that they can be completely one. Then the world will know that you sent me, and that you love them as you love me.

J 17:24   "Dear Father, you have given them to me, and I want them to be with me where I am, so that they may see my glory – the glory you gave me because you loved me, before the world was made. Oh loving, wonderful Father! The world doesn't know you. But I know you; and these men know that it was you who sent me here; and I have told them about you, and I will go on telling them, so that your love for me may be in them, and I may be in them."

M 26:36
Mk 14:32
L 22:40
J 18:1
    After saying these prayers, Jesus and his disciples walked across the ravine and crossed the brook, Kedron; and they came to a garden there called Gethsemane. Jesus had often met his disciples in this place and they knew it well; and so, of course, did Judas Iscariot.

Jesus said to his disciples, "Sit here while I go and pray; and pray that you may not fall into temptation." He took Peter and James and John with him and withdrew from them, about a stone's throw, and knelt down and prayed. Anguish and distress overwhelmed him, and he said to them, "My heart is so full of sorrow that it almost crushes me. Stay here and watch with me."

He went on a little further, and fell on his face in prayer. "My Father, all things are possible for you. Let this cup pass from me." And now there came to him an angel from heaven, bringing him strength; and in anguish of spirit he prayed the more urgently; and great drops of sweat fell from him, like drops of blood, to the ground.

When he rose from prayer and came back to the disciples he found them asleep, exhausted by their grief. "Asleep, Simon?" he said. "Couldn't you keep awake for one hour? Stay awake, all of you, and pray that you may be spared the test. The spirit is willing, but the flesh is weak."

M 26:42
Mk 14:39

Once more he went away and prayed. "Oh my Father! If this cup cannot be taken away from me unless I drink it, your will be done." On returning to his disciples he found them asleep again, for their eyes were very heavy. They did not know what to say to him.

M 26:44
Mk 14:41

A third time he went away to pray, saying the same words; and a third time he came back to them. "Still sleeping?" he said. "Still resting? Come. It's time to get up and go. The time has come for the Son of Man to be betrayed into the hands of sinful men. Look, here comes my betrayer."

L 22:47
J 18:3

Even as he spoke, Judas came into the garden. He had brought a troop of soldiers, and there were some Temple guards with them, sent by the chief priests and Pharisees. They were armed with swords and staves and carried lanterns and torches. Judas had arranged a signal. "The one I will kiss is your man," he had told them. "Seize him, and get him safely away." He walked straight up to Jesus to kiss him, but Jesus said to him, "Is it with a kiss, Judas, that you betray the Son of Man?"

J 18:4
See also
J 8:28 p. 52
Ex. 3:14

Knowing everything that was going to happen to him, Jesus stepped forward and faced the crowd. "Who is it that you are looking for?" he asked. "Jesus of Nazareth," they replied. Jesus said, "I am he." When he said, "I am he," they drew back, and fell to the ground. Again Jesus asked, "Who is it you want?" "Jesus of Nazareth," they repeated. Then Jesus said, "I have told you – 'I am he.' (« I am ») If I'm the one you want, let these others go." – thus fulfilling the words that he had spoken 'Not one of those you gave me was lost.' Then they came forward and laid hold of Jesus and held him fast.

M 26:51
Mk 14:47
L 22:49

When his disciples saw what was about to happen, they said, "Lord, shall we use our swords?" And Peter, who was carrying one of the swords, struck out wildly at the High Priest's servant and cut off his ear. The servant's name was Malchus. Jesus said to Peter,

"Enough of this! Sheathe your sword – for all who take up the sword will die by the sword. Don't you realise that I could call on my Father for help, and he would send to my aid more than twelve legions of angels? But how then would the Scripture be fulfilled which says that this must be? This is the cup my Father has given me. Do you think that I will not drink it?" And he touched the man's ear and healed him.

M 26:55
Mk 14:46

Turning to the chief priests, the Temple police and the elders who had come to arrest him, he said, "Did you have to come with swords and staves, as though I were an outlaw? I was with you in the Temple every day, and you made no attempt to arrest me. But this hour belongs to you and the powers of darkness, and the Scriptures must be fulfilled."

M 26:56
G
Mk 14:50

At this point his disciples fled. A certain young man, dressed only in a linen cloth, was following Jesus, and they tried to arrest him; but he ran away naked, leaving the linen cloth behind.

J 18:12

The troops with their commanding officer and the Jewish attendants seized Jesus and bound him, and took him first of all to Annas, father-in-law of Caiaphas, who was High Priest that year. It was Caiaphas who had advised the Jews that it would be better for them that one man should die for the people. Annas questioned Jesus about his disciples and about what he taught. Jesus answered,

J 18:19

"I have always spoken openly to everyone. All my teaching was done in the synagogue and the Temple, where all Jews meet. I have said nothing in secret; so why ask me? Why not ask the people who heard me? Ask them what I told them – they know what I said." Whereupon one of the guards struck him in the face and said, "Is that the way to answer the High Priest?" Jesus said to him, "If I have said something wrong, state it in evidence. If I spoke the truth, why strike me?" Annas sent him, still bound, to Caiaphas.

M 26:58
Mk 14:54
L 22:54
J 18:15

Peter and another disciple had followed Jesus at a distance, in an attempt to see how it all ended. This other disciple, who was acquainted with the High Priest, went into the courtyard where Jesus was being held, but Peter was stopped at the gate. So the other disciple, who knew the high Priest, went out again and had a word with the woman at the gate, and brought Peter in.

Mk 26:69

Because it was cold, the servants and the police had made a charcoal fire in the centre of the courtyard; and they all stood round it warming themselves. Peter was standing with them, sharing the warmth; and a serving maid who saw him standing in the firelight, stared at him and said, "This man was with him too." But Peter denied it. "I don't know what you mean," he said. And

about an hour later, a man said, "Yes. Of course he was with him –
he must have been – he's a Galilean!" But Peter said, "I don't know
the man you're talking about." One of the High Priest's servants, a
relative of the man whose ear Peter had cut off, insisted, "Didn't I
see you with him in the garden?" Peter swore at him. "I tell you I
don't know the man," he said. And, as he spoke, a cock crowed . . .
and Jesus turned – and looked straight at Peter. And Peter
remembered the Lord's words: 'Before cock-crow you will have
disowned me three times.'

M 26:75   And he went out – and wept bitterly.

M 26:59   When daylight came, the elders of the Jews, the chief priests
Mk 14:55   and the teachers of the Law met together in the Council, and Jesus
L 22:66   was brought before them. They tried to find some evidence against
him which would warrant the death sentence, but they failed to
find any. Many gave false evidence against him, but their
statements did not tally. Then some men stood up and perjured
themselves saying, "We heard him say, 'I will throw down this
Temple, made by human hands, and in three days I will build
another, not made with hands'." But even on this point their
evidence did not agree.

M 26:62   Then the High Priest stood up in their midst and said to Jesus,
Mk 14:60   "Have you no reply to all these accusations?" Jesus made no reply.
L 22:67   He said nothing. Again the High Priest questioned him. "In the
name of the Living God I put you on oath," he said. "Tell us, are
you the Messiah?" Jesus answered, "You will not believe me if I tell
you; and if I ask you a question you will not answer me. But you
will see the Son of Man seated at the right hand of God." They all
said, "Are you then the Christ? – the Son of the Blessed?" Jesus
Ex 3:14   replied, "As you have said. « I am » At this the High Priest tore his
robes and cried, "Blasphemy! We need call no further witnesses.
You have heard the blasphemy. What is your opinion?" "He is
guilty," they answered. "He should die."

M 26:67   The men who were guarding Jesus mocked him. They beat him,
Mk 14:65   and they blindfolded him and kept slapping him and asking, "Now,
L 22:63   prophet! Who was it hit you that time, then? Tell us that." And so
they went on, heaping insults upon him.

M 27:1   It was early in the morning when the chief priests and the Jewish
Mk 15:1   elders held consultation with the Scribes and all the Sanhedrin and
L 23:1   laid their plans against Jesus to put him to death. They put him in
J 18:28   chains and led him away and brought him before Pilate.

M 27:3   When Judas, the betrayer, saw that Jesus had been condemned
Acts 1:18 he was filled with remorse. He went to the chief priests and elders

107

and returned the thirty pieces of silver to them. "I have sinned!" he said. "I have brought an innocent man to his death." But they said, "What is that to us? That's your problem." Judas threw the money down in the Temple and left them. He went away and hanged himself.

M 27:6 The chief priests gathered up the money. "This can't be put into the Temple fund," they argued. "It's blood money." After some discussion they decided to use it to buy Potter's Field as a burial place for aliens. This explains the name 'Field of Blood' (Akeldama), by which that field has been known ever since. And Zech. 11:13 thus Jeremiah's prophecy came true: 'They took the thirty pieces of silver, the price set on a man's head – for that was his price among the Israelites – and gave the money for Potter's Field, as the Lord commanded me.'

M 27:2
J 18:28 It was still early morning when Jesus was led into the Governors' headquarters. The Jews themselves remained outside the Judgment Hall because, had they entered it, they would have become (ritually) unclean, and would not have been able to eat the Passover Feast. So Pilate came out to see them. "What charge do you bring against this man?" he asked. "If he were not a criminal," they replied, "we would not have brought him before you." Pilate said, "Take him away and try him by your own Law." "By our faith," the Jews said, "we are not permitted to execute anyone." Thus they ensured that Jesus' words would be fulfilled about the way in which he was to die.

L 23:2 "We found this man preaching subversion to the people," they said. "He opposed the payment of taxes to Caesar, and he claims M 27:11 to be the Messiah – a king." Pilate went back to the Judgment Hall J 18:33 and summoned Jesus. "Are you the king of the Jews?" he asked. Jesus said, "Is that a question of your own, or have others told you about me?" "What! Do you think I am a Jew?" said Pilate. "Your own people and their chief priests have handed you over to me. What have you done?" Jesus replied, "My Kingdom doesn't belong to this world. If it did, my followers would even now be fighting to prevent me from being arrested by the Jews." "You are M 27:12 a king, then?" "King is your word," Jesus answered, "I have come to bear witness to the Truth. That is why I was born – why I came into the world; and everyone who knows the truth when he hears it, listens to my voice." "But – what is truth?" said Pilate.

The chief priests brought many accusations against Jesus. He Mk 15:3 said nothing, however, in answer to them. Pilate questioned him again. "Have you nothing to say in your defence? Don't you hear all these charges they are bringing against you?" But, to Pilate's astonishment, Jesus made no further reply.

L 23:4 Pilate then returned to the chief priests and the crowd. "I find no case for this man to answer," he said. But they insisted: "His teaching is stirring up the people. He started in Galilee, went through the whole of Judea, and now he's here in Jerusalem." Pilate immediately asked if the man was a Galilean, and on learning that he came under Herod's jurisdiction, he sent him at once to Herod, who was in Jerusalem for the Passover.

L 23:8 Herod was greatly delighted to see Jesus. He had long wanted to see him because he had heard about him, and also because he hoped to see him perform some miracle. But though he put many questions to him, Jesus gave no answer; and the chief priests and lawyers stepped forward and started making strong accusations against him. Then Herod and his men scoffed at Jesus, and treated him with ridicule and contempt. They sent him back to Pilate, dressed in a gorgeous purple robe. Pilate and Herod became friends that day. Until that time, there had been a long-standing feud between them.

M 27:19 While Pilate was sitting in the Judgment Hall, his wife sent him a message: "Have nothing to do with that innocent man, I was much troubled on his account in my dreams last night."

M 27:15
Mk 15:6
I 23:13
J 18:39 Pilate called together the chief priests, the elders and the people. "You brought this man to me on a charge of subversion," he said. "As far as I am concerned he is not guilty of any crime. I have examined him myself in your presence and found nothing to support your charges. No more did Herod, for he sent him back to me. Clearly he has done nothing to deserve death. I therefore propose to let him off with a flogging. Now, according to one of your customs, I always set a prisoner free for you at Passover. Why not let me release this 'King of the Jews' for you?" – for he realised that it was out of spite that they had brought Jesus before him. But the chief priests had stirred up the crowd to shout for Jesus-Barabbas. "No! Not him!" they yelled. "Free Barabbas!" Jesus-Barabbas was a notorious bandit, in prison at that time, with other rebels, for murder.

M 27:27
Mk 15:16
J 19:1 Pilate now ordered Jesus to be flogged. He was taken to the guardroom, where he was surrounded by all the Praetorium soldiers. They stripped him, threw the purple robe around him, plaited a 'crown' of thorns and put it on his head, put a stick in his right hand and knelt before him in mock homage, chanting "Hail! King of the Jews!" They spat upon him, and used the stick to beat

him about the head. And they flogged him.

M 27:21
J 19:4
Once more Pilate stood before the Jews. "Here he is!" he cried. "I am bringing him out to you to show why I can find no case against him." And Jesus came out, wearing the crown of thorns and the purple robe. "Behold the man!" said Pilate. "Now, which do you want me to set free for you – Jesus-Barabbas, or Jesus-called-Messiah?" As soon as the chief priests saw Jesus, they shouted, "Crucify! Crucify him!" "But what crime has he committed?" asked Pilate. "Take him away and crucify him yourselves. For my part, I can find no case against him." The Jews answered, "We have a law, and by that law he ought to die because he claims to be the Son of God."

J 19:8
When Pilate heard this, he was more afraid than ever. He went back into the Judgment Hall and asked Jesus, "Where have you come from?" But Jesus gave him no answer. "Do you refuse to speak to me?" said Pilate. "Don't you know that I have the authority to release you – and also to crucify you?" Jesus replied, "You have no authority over me unless it is given to you by God. And, therefore, worse guilt lies with the man who handed me over to you."

J 19:12
On hearing these words, Pilate was even more anxious to release him. But the Jews shouted, "If you let this man go, you are no friend of Caesar's! Any man who claims to be a king is defying Caesar!" Pilate heard what they were saying, and he brought Jesus outside and took his judge's seat at the place known as 'The Pavement' – Gabbatha – in the language of the Jews. It was Passover eve.

Pilate said to the Jews, "Here is your king!" And, for the third time, he said to them, "I have not found him guilty of any capital offence." But they kept shouting, "Away with him! Away with him! Crucify him!"

"Crucify your King?" said Pilate.

"We have no king but Caesar!" they cried.

M 27:24
Pilate saw that it was useless to go on. In fact, a riot was brewing. So he took some water and ceremoniously washed his hands in front of all the people. "My hands are clean of this man's blood," he said. "This is your affair." And, with one voice, the people cried, "His blood be on us, and on our children!"

M 27:31
Mk 15:15
L 23:24
J 19:16
J 19:17
Then he released to them the man they wanted, the one who had been sent to prison for rioting and murder, and he handed Jesus over to them to be crucified. The soldiers (the four who made up the crucifixion party) took off the purple robe and dressed Jesus in his own clothes – and then led him out to be nailed to the

cross. He went out carrying his own cross.

M 27:32   On their way to the place of crucifixion they met a man called Simon, of Cyrene, father of Alexander and Rufus. He was passing by on his way into the city from the country, and the soldiers pressed him into service. They made him walk behind Jesus carrying the cross on his back.

L 23:27   A large crowd of people followed him. There were many women among them who mourned and lamented over him. He turned to them and said, "Daughters of Jerusalem, don't weep for me; weep for yourselves and your children. For the days are surely coming when people will say, 'Blessed are the barren! – the wombs that have never borne a child, the breasts that have never

Hos. 10:8 suckled!' – when people will say to the mountains, 'Fall on us!' and to the hills, 'cover us!' For if these things are done when the wood is green, what will be done when it is dry?"

M 27:38
Mk 15:27
L 23:32
J 19:18

    There were two others with him – criminals who were to be put to death with Jesus. They were taken to a place called 'Golgotha,' which means 'Place of the skull.' There they offered Jesus wine to drink, mixed with myrrh; but after tasting it, he would not drink it.

L 23:34   And there they nailed him to the cross. And Jesus prayed, "Father, forgive them. They don't understand what they are doing." They nailed the criminals to the crosses beside Jesus, one on his right and one on his left. Thus was the Scripture fulfilled

Mk 15:28
Isa. 53:12
M 27:37
Mk 15:26
L 23:38
J 19:19

which says; 'He was classed with criminals.'
    Pilate had written the inscription giving the charge, to be fastened to the cross. It read: 'JESUS OF NAZARETH, KING OF THE JEWS." This inscription was read by many Jews because the place where Jesus was crucified was not far from the city; and the inscription was written in Hebrew and in Latin and in Greek. The Jewish chief priests said to Pilate, "Do not write: 'The King of the Jews.' You should write: 'This man claimed that he was King of the Jews.'" But Pilate answered, "What I have written, I have written."

Mk 15:25   It was nine o'clock in the morning when they crucified him.

M 27:35
Mk 15:24
L 23:35
J 19:23
Psa. 22

    After the soldiers had crucified Jesus, they took possession of his clothes. They divided them into four parts, one for each soldier – except for Jesus' robe. The robe was seamless; it had been made from one piece of woven cloth. They said to each other, 'It'd be a pity to tear it. Let's throw the dice and see who wins it." And so it was that the text in the Scriptures came true: They distributed my clothes among them, and drew lots for my raiment. That is precisely what the soldiers did. Then they sat down to keep watch.

M 27:39
Mk 15:29
L 23:35

Some of the crowd just stood and stared. Some of the Jewish leaders mocked him: "He saved others," they said; "Let him save himself – if he is God's Messiah – the Chosen One!" Passers-by hurled abuse at him: "Aha!" they cried, wagging their heads. "You would pull the Temple down, would you? – and build it again in three days? Why don't you come down from the cross and save yourself?" And the soldiers mocked him; they came forward offering their sour wine. "If you are King of the Jews," they said, "save yourself." So, too, doctors of the Law and chief priests joked

Mk 15:32

together. "He saved others," they said, "but he can't save himself! Let this Messiah, this King of Israel, come down from the cross! If we see that, we will believe!" "He trusts in God – and says he's God's Son. Well then, let's see if God wants to save him now!"

L 23:39

Even one of the bandits who were crucified with him taunted him: "You're the Messiah, aren't you? Save yourself – and us as

M 27:44

well!" But the other bandit said, "Aren't you afraid – even of God? We are all here under the same sentence. For us it's plain justice – we're only getting what we deserve. But him – he's done nothing wrong." And he said, "Jesus, remember me when you come into your Kingdom." Jesus said to him, "I tell you – this very day you will be with me in Paradise."

J 19:25
Mk 15:40
M 27:56

Near Jesus' cross stood his mother, with her sister, Salome, and Mary, wife of Clopas and Mary of Magdala, from whom Jesus had once cast out seven devils. Jesus saw his mother, with the disciple whom he loved standing beside her. He said to her, "Mother, there is your son." And to the disciple he said, "There is your mother." And from that time, the disciple took Mary to live with him in his own house.

M 27:45
2 Cor 5:21
Psa. 22
Mk 15:33
L 23:44
M 27:47
Mk 15:36
J 19:28

At about midday the sun was eclipsed; and darkness covered the whole country until three o'clock. Then Jesus cried out in a loud voice « Eli, Eli, lama sabachthani? » – « My God, why has thou forsaken me? » Some of the people standing there heard him, and they said, "He is calling for Elijah."

Again in fulfilment of the Scriptures, Jesus said, "I'm thirsty." And one of them ran at once and fetched a sponge which he soaked in sour wine, put it on the end of a branch of hyssop, and held it to Jesus' lips. But the others said, "Wait! Let's see if Elijah will come and save him."

L 23:46
J 19:30

Jesus received the wine and, knowing that he had fulfilled every last prophecy, and that he had completed each and every work that he had come to do, he cried aloud, "It is finished! Father, into your hands I commend my Spirit." And he bowed his head, and he died.

M 27:51
Mk 15:38

The veil of the Temple was torn in two from top to bottom. There was an earthquake. Rocks split asunder and graves were broken open, and many of God's people rose from sleep; and, coming out of their graves after his resurrection, they went into the Holy City, where many saw them.

M 27:54
Mk 15:39
L 23:47

And when the centurion and the men who were on watch with him, saw the earthquake and everything else that happened, they were filled with wonder. The centurion had been standing there, in front of the cross, when Jesus cried out and died; and he said, "This man was, in truth, the Son of God."

When the people who had gathered to watch the spectacle saw what happened, they all went home, beating their breasts.

Mk 15:40

Many of Jesus' friends had been standing at a distance; the women who had accompanied him from Galilee stood with them and saw all these things. Among them, besides Mary of Magdala, there were Mary, the mother of James the Younger and of Joseph; and Salome, the mother of the sons of Zebedee. They had all followed him and waited on him when he was in Galilee. And there were several others who had come up to Jerusalem with him.

J 19:31

Because it was Preparation Day – the eve of the Sabbath – the Jews were anxious that the bodies should not remain on the crosses, especially as the Passover Sabbath was a day of particular solemnity. So they asked Pilate to order that the legs be broken and the bodies removed. The soldiers went to each of the men who had been crucified with Jesus, and broke their legs. But when they came to Jesus, they found that he was already dead; so they did not break his legs. But one of the soldiers stabbed his side with a spear; and at once blood and water flowed from the wound. This is vouched for by an eye-witness whose evidence is to be trusted. We know what he said is true, and he also knows that he speaks the truth, so that you also may believe. This was done to

Ex. 12:46
Zech. 12:10

fulfil the Scripture: 'No bone of his shall be broken' and another which says: 'They shall look on him whom they pierced.'

M 27:57
Mk 15:42
L 23:50
J 19:38

It was getting towards evening when Joseph of Arimathea arrived. He was a good man, who had always looked for the coming of the Kingdom of God. He was rich, and a respected member of the Council, though he had dissented from their policy and the action they had taken. He himself had become a disciple of Jesus – but secretly, for fear of the Jews. This man now bravely approached Pilate and asked to be allowed to remove Jesus' body. Pilate was surprised to hear that Jesus had died so soon. He sent for the centurion and asked him the time of death. When he heard the centurion's report he gave permission to Joseph to take the dead body.

M 27:59

Joseph went and bought a linen sheet. He was joined by Nicodemus, the man who had first visited Jesus by night. Nicodemus had brought with him more than half a hundredweight of a mixture of myrrh and aloes. Together they took the body of Jesus down from the cross and wrapped it, with the spices, in strips of the linen, as was the custom in Jewish burials. Now, in the place of crucifixion there was a garden, and in the garden was a tomb, newly cut out of the rock. It was Joseph's own tomb and had never as yet been used for burial. There, because it was Passover Eve, and because it was close at hand, they laid the body. Then they rolled the great stone across the door of the tomb, and went away. Mary of Magdala was there, and the other Mary, sitting opposite to the grave, and they saw where he was laid. Then they went home and prepared spices and perfumes.

M 27:62

The following day – the day after the Preparation – the chief priests and the Pharisees went to visit Pilate. "Your Excellency," they said, "we remember how, while he was alive, that impostor said, 'After three days I will rise from the dead.' So will you give orders for the grave to be securely guarded until the third day? – so that his disciples cannot steal the body, and then tell everyone that he has risen from the dead: and the final deception would then be worse than the first." "You may have your guard," said Pilate. "Go, and make it secure as best you can." So they left, and made the grave secure by putting a seal on the stone, and leaving sentries on watch.

L 23:56

In accordance with the Law, the Passover Sabbath was observed as a day of rest.

M 28:1
Mk 16:1
L 24:1
J 20:1

At sunrise on Sunday, Mary of Magdala, Mary, the mother of James, Joanna, Salome and others, brought aromatic oils and spices to anoint the body of Jesus. As they walked to the tomb, they were wondering who might roll the great stone away from the entrance for them. Then, as they approached the tomb, there was another earth tremor; and an angel of the Lord descended from heaven. He came to the stone and rolled it away from the tomb, and sat himself down upon it. His face shone like lightning; and his robes were white as snow. At the sight of him the guards shook with fear and lay on the ground like dead men. The women too were extremely frightened ; but the angel said, "You mustn't be afraid. I know that you are looking for Jesus of Nazareth, who was crucified. But why are you looking for the living among the dead? He is not here. He has been raised from death. See, here is the place where they laid him. Remember what he said when he was in Galilee: 'The Son of Man must be given up into the power of sinful men, and be crucified; and be raised to life on the third day.' Go and give this message to Peter and the disciples: 'He is going to Galilee before you, as he promised, and he will see you there.' That is the message I was to give you."

M 28:7

Mk 16:7

L 24:5

The women were so terrified that they stood with their heads bowed, not daring to look up. Then they ran from the tomb; and they spoke to no one because they were so frightened. Yet even so their hearts were full of joy. They went to Peter and the disciples and delivered the instructions briefly to them. Mary said, "They have taken the Lord from the tomb, and we don't know where they have laid him." To the disciples they seemed to be talking nonsense; but Peter and the other disciple whom Jesus loved set out and they ran to the tomb. They were running together, but as they approached the garden, the other disciple was running faster than Peter, and so reached the tomb first. He stooped and looked inside. He saw the linen wrappings lying there, but he did not go in. Then Simon Peter came up behind him; and he went inside and saw the linen cloths; and the cloth that had been placed round Jesus' head was lying, rolled up, separately, in a place by itself. Then the other disciple went in to the tomb and, as he looked at these things, he realised what had happened. But as yet they did not understand the meaning of the Scripture which said that Jesus was to rise from the dead. And they went home.

J 20:2

But Mary Magdalene remained outside the tomb weeping. Still crying, she stooped and looked into the tomb; and there she saw two angels, robed in shinning white, seated – one at the head and one at the foot of the place where Jesus had lain. They spoke to her: "Woman, why are you weeping?" She said, "Because they have taken away my Lord, and I don't know where they have laid him." Then she looked (over her shoulder) and saw Jesus standing there; but she did not see that it was Jesus. He said to her "Woman, why are you crying?" Thinking that perhaps he was the gardener, she cried, "Oh sir, if it was you who moved him, tell me where you have laid him and I will take him away." Jesus said, "Mary!" She turned to face him. "Rabboni!" she cried. Jesus said to her, "No, don't cling to me, for I have not yet ascended to my Father. But go

J 20:11

Mk 16:9

G

115

to my brothers and tell them for me: 'I am going back to him who is my Father, and your Father; my God and your God.' "

So Mary went to find the disciples, who were still mourning and sorrowful. "I've seen him!" she said; and she gave them his message. But they did not believe it.

M 28:11 Meanwhile some of the men who had been on guard duty at the grave went into the city to the chief priests and reported everything that had happened. After meeting and conferring with the elders, the chief priests gave the men a considerable sum of money and told them to say: "His disciples came in the night and stole the body while we slept." "If this should come to the Governor's ears," they added, "we will put matters right with him. You won't get into trouble." So they took the money and did as they were told. And this is the account given by many Jews to this day.

Mk 16:12 That same day, two of the disciples were talking over all these
L 24:13 events while on their way to a village called Emmaus, about seven miles from Jerusalem. And as they were discussing it together, Jesus himself came up and walked along with them; but something prevented them from recognising him. He said to them, "What is it that you are debating on your walk?" They stopped, looking very dejected, and one of them, Cleopas, answered, "You must be the only man alive in Jerusalem who doesn't know what has been happening here in the last few days!" "What things?" Jesus asked. "Why, all this about Jesus of Nazareth," they said. "This man was a prophet and was, to God, and to all the people, mighty in words and deeds. Our chief priests and our rulers handed him over to be sentenced to death, and crucified him. And we had hoped that he

G would be the One who was going to redeem Israel. But, what is more, this is the third day since it happened and now some of the women of our company have amazed us; they went early to the tomb, and failed to find his body. They returned with a story that they had seen a vision of angels who told them that he was alive. Some of our people went to the tomb and found things just as the women had said; but him – they did not see." "O foolish men!" Jesus said. "With hearts so slow to believe, after all the prophets have told you! Was not the Messiah bound to suffer like that before entering upon his glory?" Then, beginning with Moses and the prophets, he explained to them all the passages of the Scriptures which referred to himself.

By this time they had reached the village of Emmaus and Jesus made as if to continue along the road. But they said, "Stay with us. It's getting late – the day's almost over." So he went in to stay with them. And when he sat down at table with them, he took bread and said the blessing. He broke the bread and he offered it to them. Then their eyes were opened, and they knew who he was – and he vanished from their sight. They said to each other, "Didn't we feel our hearts on fire when he was talking to us along the road? – and when he explained the Scriptures to us?"

L 24:33
J 20:19

Without a moment's delay they got up and set off on the journey back to Jerusalem. It was late in the evening when they arrived in the city and found the disciples gathered together. The doors were shut and locked for fear of the Jews. The disciples said to them, "It's true! The Lord is risen! He has appeared to Simon!" Then the two who had just returned from Emmaus told them all about the events of their journey and how they had recognised Jesus as he was breaking the bread.

They were talking about all this when – there was Jesus himself, standing in their midst. "Peace be with you!" He said to them. They were startled and terrified, imagining that it was a ghost they were seeing. But he said, "Why are you so confused? Why all these questions in your minds? Look at my hands, and my feet. It is I

J 20:20

myself. Touch me and see – a ghost doesn't have flesh and bones, as you can see I have!" And he showed them his hands and his feet. But they were still incredulous, for it seemed too wonderful to be true. So he asked them, "Have you anything here to eat?" They offered him a piece of fish which they had cooked, which he took and ate as they

Mk 16:14

watched him; and he reproached them for their incredulity, and their slowness to believe those who had seen him risen from the dead. "These are the very things I told you about," he said, "while I was still with you, that everything that was written about me in the Law and

L 24:45

the Prophets was bound to be fulfilled." And he opened their minds so that they could understand the Scriptures, where it is written that the Messiah must suffer and be raised from death on the third day; and that in his name the message about repentance and forgiveness of sins must be preached to all the nations of the earth.

Then the disciples were filled with joy at seeing the Lord. "Peace be with you," he said again. And he said "As the Father has sent me, so I send you." Then he breathed on them, and said, "Receive the Holy Spirit. If you forgive any man's sins, they stand forgiven. If you do not forgive them, unforgiven they remain."

J 20:24

One of the eleven, Thomas, known as the 'Twin', was not with the rest when Jesus came. The disciples told him, "We have seen the Lord!" But Thomas said, "Unless I see his hands, with the marks of the nails, and put my finger where the nails were, and my hand

117

into his side – I'll not believe it."

J 20:26   A week later, the disciples were again in that room, and Thomas was with them. Although the doors, again, were locked, Jesus came and stood among them. "Peace be with you," he said. Then he turned to Thomas, "Look at my hands, Thomas" he said. "Put your finger here, and put your hand into my side – and be unbelieving no more, but believe." And Thomas said, "My Lord! and my God!" Jesus said, "Because you have seen me, you have found faith. Happy are those who have never seen me, and yet have found faith!"

M 28:16   (The disciples made their way back to Galilee; and) it was some
J 21:1   time later that Jesus showed himself to them by the Sea of Galilee. It happened in this way:

J 21:2   Seven of the disciples were together on the sea-shore. They were Simon Peter, Thomas the 'Twin', Nathaniel from Cana-in-Galilee, the sons of Zebedee, and two others. Simon Peter said, "I'm going fishing!" "We'll come too," said the others; and they all got into the boat and off they went. But, though they fished all night, they caught nothing. As the sun was rising, they saw a man standing on the distant shore. It was Jesus, though they did not realise it. He called to them. "Haven't you caught anything, my friends?" "Nothing!" they called back. "Cast your net on the right hand side of the boat," he said, "and you'll catch some." So they threw the net out, but when they came to pull it in, they could not get it aboard for the weight of fish in it. Then the disciple whom Jesus loved said to Peter, "It's the Lord!" When Simon Peter heard that, he put on his clothes because he had stripped for the fishing – and plunged into the sea. The rest of them came ashore in the boat, pulling the net full of fish with them. They were not far from the shore – only about a hundred yards.

    As they came ashore they saw a charcoal fire burning there, with fish and bread laid on it. Jesus said, "Bring some of the fish you have caught." Simon Peter went aboard and dragged the net ashore. It was full of big fish – a hundred and fifty-three of them – yet, for all their weight, the net did not break. Jesus said to them, "Come and eat." Nobody dared to ask, "Who are you?" – they all knew who it was. Then Jesus came up, and he took the bread and gave it to them, and the fish also.

J 21:14   This was the third time that Jesus had appeared to his apostles after his resurrection.

    After they had finished breakfast, Jesus said to Simon Peter,

"Simon, son of John, do you love me more than all others?" "Yes, Lord," answered Simon. "You know that I love you." "Then feed my lambs," Jesus said. Again Jesus said to him, "Simon, son of John, do you love me?" "Yes, Lord, you know that I love you," he answered. And Jesus said to him, "Feed my sheep." Then, for the third time, Jesus asked him, "Simon, son of John, do you love me?" Peter was grieved that Jesus should ask him a third time. He said, "Lord, you know everything; you know that I love you." Jesus said to him, "Feed my sheep. And I'll tell you something, Peter: when you were young, you buckled on your belt and walked where you chose, but when you are old, you will stretch out your arms, and a stranger will bind them fast, and carry you where you don't want to go." Thus he prophesied the way in which Peter would die to bring glory to God. Then he said, "Follow me."

J21:20 Peter looked round and saw the disciple whom Jesus loved, following – the one who at supper had leaned close to Jesus and asked, "Lord, who is it that will betray you?" When Peter saw him, he said, "Lord, what is to happen to him?" Jesus said, "If I should wish that he wait until I come, what is that to you? Follow me."

Those words of Jesus' were noted by his disciples, and they were taken to mean that that disciple would not die. Jesus did not actually say that he would not die, but only: "If I should wish that he wait until I come, what is that to you?"

It is this same disciple who confirms what has here been written – in fact, it is he who wrote it; and we know that his testimony is true.

J 20:30 There were indeed many other signs that Jesus performed in the presence of his disciples which are not recorded in this book. Those written here have been recorded in order that you may hold the faith that Jesus is the Christ, the Son of God, and that through this faith you may possess eternal life by his name.

Acts 1:3 During the forty days following his resurrection Jesus appeared to them many times, and taught them about the Kingdom of God.

M 28:18 A few days before the Feast of Pentecost the apostles were all in Jerusalem. Jesus said to them, "Full authority in heaven and on earth has been given to me. Go then to all the peoples of the earth and make them my disciples. Baptise them in the name of the Father, and of the Son and of the Holy Spirit; and teach them to obey all the commands I have given you. And remember, I am with you always, to the end of time."

Mk 16:15 Through his disciples, Jesus sent out the sacred and ever-living
& additional message of eternal salvation. He told them that in his name, this
paragraph message about repentance and forgiveness of sins must be

Mk 16:16 preached to all the nations of the earth. "Those who believe it," he said, "and receive baptism, will find salvation. Those who do not believe it will be condemned.

"And for those who believe, these miracles will follow: they will cast out demons in my name; they will speak in foreign tongues; if they handle snakes, or drink any deadly poison, they will come to no harm; and the sick upon whom they lay their hands will recover.

L 24:49 "Begin in Jerusalem. It is you who are witnesses to all this. And remember, I myself will send you my Father's promised gift. So stay here in Jerusalem until you are armed with the power from above. John, as you know, baptised with water; but, in a few days,

Acts 1:8 you will be baptised with the Holy Spirit. And when the Holy Spirit comes upon you, you will be filled with power. And you will be witnesses for me in Jerusalem, and throughout Judea and Samaria, and to the ends of the earth."

L 24:50 Then he led them out of the city as far as Bethany, and he blessed them with uplifted hands; and in the act of blessing them, he parted from them. He was taken up to heaven as they watched, and a mist hid him from their sight.

Mk 16:19 Jesus Christ, the Lord, was taken up into heaven, and he took his place at the right hand of God.

Acts 1:10 And they were all staring up at the sky, trying to see him, when, suddenly, there stood beside them two men robed in white, who said, "Men of Galilee! Why stand there looking up at the sky? This very same Jesus who has been taken away from you up to heaven, will come again – in the same way as you have seen him go." This was on the Mount of Olives – at Bethany.

L 24:52
Acts 1:12 They all returned to Jerusalem with great joy. It was not very far – about a Sabbath day's journey. They went into the city – to the first floor room, where they were all staying – Peter and John, James and Andrew, Philip and Thomas, Bartholomew (Nathaniel) and Matthew, James – Alphaeus' son, Simon – the Zealot, and Judas – James' son – also called Thaddaeus. All these prayed together constantly; and with them were Jesus' brothers and a group of women including Mary, the mother of Jesus. And they were continually in the Temple, praising God.

Mk 16:20 They went out to proclaim the Gospel everywhere; and the Lord worked with them, and confirmed their words by the miracles that followed.

J 21:25 There is much else that Jesus did. But if it were all recorded in detail, I suppose the whole world could not hold all the books that would be written.

APPENDIX

Words not included in the main text

M 1:1-18
L 3:23-38

The line of descent – Adam to Joseph. Please see page (xxxvi) and page 12.

M 21:18
Mk 11:12
and 20

The cursed fig tree. It is hard to accept that, in the first place, Jesus would ever look for figs when they were out of season and if he did that, finding none, he would curse the fig tree! Perhaps the account was incomplete; or could it be that, as with the end of Mark's gospel, something happened to it? It is also thought possible that this story may have been told originally as a parable.

The last paragraph is, of course, of the greatest importance:

'The next day, as they were returning from Bethany, Jesus was hungry. He saw in the distance a fig tree covered with leaves and he went to see if he could find any figs on it. But when he came to it he found only leaves because it was not the time of year for figs. Jesus said to the tree, "No one shall ever eat figs from you again!" His disciples heard him say it.

'Early the next morning, as they walked the same road, they saw the fig tree. It was dead from the roots up. Peter, remembering what had happened, said to Jesus, "Look, Rabbi! The fig tree you cursed has died."

'Jesus said, "Have faith in God. I tell you, if anyone says to this mountain, 'Get up – and cast yourself into the sea!' and has no doubt in his mind that what he says will happen, it will be done for him. For this reason I tell you: when you pray and ask for something, believe that you have received it, and everything will be given to you."'

L 1:1-4

The introduction to Luke's gospel – see also page (i) Supplementary Notes.

'The author to Theophilus: Many writers have undertaken to write accounts of the events that have taken place among us. They have written of the things told to us by the original eyewitnesses and servants of the Gospel. And so, your Excellency, because I have carefully studied all these matters from their beginning, I have decided to write an orderly account for you, to give you the full truth of the matters about which you have been informed.'

L 2:39   "... to their own town of Nazareth." Luke does not give accounts of the magi and the flight into Egypt.

J 19:14   The words: 'And about the sixth hour' – have been omitted in favour of Mark 15:25. See page 111. John probably uses the Roman concept of time, while Mark uses the Jewish.

ST MATTHEW

IN THE FOUR GOSPELS AS ONE

Chap	Verse	Page	Chap	Verse	Page	Chap	Verse	Page
1	1-17	xxxvi	8	1-4	21	12	33	27
	18-20	4		5-9	28		34-37	31
	21-25	5		10-13	29		38-50	32
2	1-17	7		14-17	19	13	1-10	33
	18-23	8		18-22	36		11-23	34
3	1-2	9		23-34	37		24-43	35
	3	11	9	1-5	21		44-46	36
	4-10	9		6-17	22		47-50	35
	11-12	11		18-24	38		51-52	36
	13-14	9		25-31	39		53-54	19
	15-17	10		32-34	31		55-58	20
4	1-11	10		35-38	29	14	1-2	59
	12-17	20	10	1-4	33		3-5	20
	18-22	13		5-15	43		6-13	45
	23-25	21		16	67		14-25	46
5	1-2	22		17-22	91		26-36	47
	3-22	23		23-25	44	15	1-2	57
	23-45	24		26-27	36		3-22	58
	46-48	25		28-31	44		23-31	59
6	1-13	26		32-33	32		32-39	60
	14-18	27		34-39	44	16	1-12	60
	19-21	25		40-42	32		13-25	61
	22-23	36	11	1	33		26-28	62
	24-25	25		2-15	39	17	1-13	62
	26-34	26		16-24	40		14-23	63
7	1-5	25		25-30	70		24-27	64
	6-16	27	12	1-18	30	18	1-7	64
	17-28	28		19-32	31		8-9	24
							10	64

ST MATTHEW

IN THE FOUR GOSPELS AS ONE

Chap	Verse	Page	Chap	Verse	Page	Chap	Verse	Page
18	11	80	24	14	92	27	1	107
	12-14	65		15-18	91		2	108
	15-22	66		19-22	92		3	107
	23-35	67		23-27	91		4-14	108
19	1-15	68		28-36	92		15-21	109
	16-30	69		37-39	93		22-26	110
20	1-5	69		40-42	92		27-30	109
	6-16	70		43-51	73		31	110
	17-19	78	25	1-13	93		32-38	111
	20-28	79		14-28	80		39-49	112
	(29-34)	79		29-30	81		50-58	113
21	1-2	83		31-32	93		59-66	114
	3-9	84		33-46	94	28	1-4	114
	10-11	85	26	3-5	82		5-10	115
	12-13	14		6-13	83		11-15	116
	14-15	86		14-16	94		16-17	118
	16-17	87		17-20	96		18-20	119
	18-22	Appx		21-22	97			
	23-38	85		23-25	98			
	39-46	86		26-29	96			
22	1-14	86		30	98			
	15-32	87		31-35	99			
	33-46	88		36-38	104			
23	1-12	88		39-51	105			
	13-33	89		52-58	106			
	34-39	90		59-68	107			
24	1-6	90		69-70	106			
	7-13	91		71-75	107			

ST MARK

IN THE FOUR GOSPELS AS ONE

Chap	Verse	Page	Chap	Verse	Page	Chap	Verse	Page
1	1	1	7	5-25	58	14	3-9	83
	2-3	11		26-37	59		10-11	94
	4-6	9	8	1-10	60		12-17	96
	7-8	11		11-21	60		18-19	97
	9-13	10		22-35	61		20-21	98
	14-15	20		36-38	62		22-23	96
	16-20	13	9	1-13	62		24	97
	21-27	18		14-31	63		25	96
	28-39	19		32-42	64		26	98
	40-45	21		43-48	24		27-31	99
2	1-9	21		49-50	23		32-33	104
	10-22	22	10	1-16	68		34-47	105
	23-28	30		17-31	69		48-54	106
3	1-6	30		32-34	78		55-65	107
	7-19	33		35-52	79		66-68	106
	20-30	31	11	1-2	83		69-72	107
	31-35	32		3-10	84	15	1	107
4	1-10	33		11	85		2-5	108
	11-20	34		12-14	Appx		6-11	109
	21-23	36		15-18	14		12-15	110
	24-25	25		19	85		16-19	109
	26-29	34		20-24	Appx		20	110
	30-31	35		25-26	27		21-28	111
	35-41	37		27-33	85		29-36	112
5	1-18	37	12	1-8	85		37-43	113
	19-40	38		9-12	86		44-47	114
	41-43	39		13-27	87	16	1-5	114
6	1-2	19		28-40	88		6-9	115
	3-6	20		41-44	90		10-13	116
	7-11	43	13	1-7	90		14	117
	12-13	45		8-16	91		15	119
	14-16	59		17-20	92		16-20	120
	17-32	45		21-23	91			
	33-48	46		24-32	92			
	49-56	47		33-37	93			
7	1-4	57	14	1-2	82			

ST LUKE

IN THE FOUR GOSPELS AS ONE

Chap	Verse	Page	Chap	Verse	Page	Chap	Verse	Page
1	1-4	Appx	6	27-31	24	9	51-56	78
	5-7	1		32-42	25		57-62	36
	8-29	2		43-44	28	10	1-9	67
	30-60	3		45	31		10-12	68
	61-80	4		46-49	28		13-15	40
2	1-19	5	7	1-8	28		16	43
	20-39	6		9-17	29		17-22	70
	40-52	8		18-28	39		23-42	71
3	1-15	9		29-35	40	11	(1)	
	16-17	11		36-42	42		2-4	26
	18	9		43-50	43		5-13	27
	19-20	20	8	1-3	43		14-23	31
	21-22	10		4-9	33		24-32	32
	23-38	12		10-15	34		33	23
4	1-13	10		16	23		34-36	36
	14-15	12		17-18	36		37	71
	16-22	19		19-21	32		38-41	72
	23-30	20		22-37	37		42	89
	31-36	18		38-51	38		43	88
	37-44	19		52-56	39		44	89
5	1-3	12	9	1-5	43		45-46	88
	4-11	13		6	45		47-49	89
	12-23	21		7-9	59		50-51	90
	24-39	22		10	45		52	89
6	1-11	30		11-17	46		53-54	72
	12-16	33		18-24	61	12	1	60
	17-19	21		25-36	62		2-3	36
	20-23	23		37-44	63		4-7	44
	(24-26 reverse)			45-50	64		8-9	32

ST LUKE

IN THE FOUR GOSPELS AS ONE

Chap	Verse	Page	Chap	Verse	Page	Chap	Verse	Page
12	10	31	16	18	24	20	39-46	88
	11-12	91		19-30	76		47	89
	13-21	72		31	77	21	1-9	90
	22	25	17	1-2	64		10-21	91
	23-31	26		3-4	66		22-33	92
	32-37	72		5 6	63		34-36	93
	38-48	73		7-21	77		37-38	94
	49-53	44		22	90	22	(1) 2	86
	54-56	60		23-25	91		3-6	94
	57-59	24		26-30	93		7-20	96
13	1-9	73		31-34	91		21-31	98
	10-17	74		35-37	92		32-38	99
	18-21	35	18	1-7	77		39-41	104
	22-24	27		8-14	78		42-50	105
	25-30	29		15-17	68		51-57	106
	31	78		18-30	69		58-71	107
	32-33	79		31-34	78	23	1	107
	34-35	90		35-43	79		2-4	108
14	1-12	74	19	1-25	80		5-19	109
	13-24	75		26-27	81		20-25	110
	25-33	44		28-30	83		26-34	111
	34-35	23		31-44	84		35-46	112
15	1-20	65		45 48	14		47-52	113
	21-32	66	20	1-15	85		53 56	114
16	1-8	75		16-19	86	24	1-4	114
	9-17	76		20-38	87		5-12	115
							13 29	116
							30-49	117
							50-53	120

ST JOHN

IN THE FOUR GOSPELS AS ONE

Chap	Verse	Page	Chap	Verse	Page	Chap	Verse	Page
1	1-14	1	8	1-7	51	16	1-21	102
	15	11		8-28	52		22-33	103
	16-18	1		29-52	53	17	1-10	103
	19-21	10		53-59	54		11-26	104
	22-42	11	9	1-16	54	18	1-2	104
	43-51	12		17-40	55		3-11	105
2	1-11	13		41	56		12-25	106
	12-25	14	10	1-21	56		26-28	107
3	1-2	14		22-42	57		28-38	108
	3-26	15	11	1-28	81		39-40	109
	27-36	16		29-54	82	19	1-3	109
4	1-13	16		55-57	83		4-16	110
	14-38	17	12	1-11	83		17-24	111
	39-54	18		12-19	84		25-30	112
5	1-9	40		20-22	94		31-38	113
	10-30	41		23-43	95		39-42	114
	31-47	42		44-50	96	20	1	114
6	1	42	13	1	96		2-17	115
	2-19	46		2-23	97		18	116
	20-33	47		24-36	98		19-25	117
	34-58	48		37-38	99		25-29	118
	59-71	49	14	1-13	99		30-31	119
7	1-15	49		14-31	100	21	1-15	118
	16-36	50	15	1-3	100		15-24	119
	37-52	51		4-27	101		25	120

PEOPLE

		Page
A	Andrew	11, 33, 46, 90, 120
	Anna	6
	Annas	9, 106
	Archelaus	8
	Augustus (Roman Emperor)	5
	Barabbas (Jesus-Barabbas)	109, 110
A	Bartholomew (see Nathaniel)	12, 33, 120
	Bartimaeus	79
	Caiaphas	9, 82, 106, 107
	Cleopas	116
	Elijah	9, 20, 59, 62, 78
	Elizabeth	1-3
	Gabriel, archangel	2, 3, 4, 5, 8
	Gadarenes	37
	Herod the Great	1, 7, 8
	Herod Antipas	9, 20, 45, 59, 79, 109
	Herodias	20, 45
	Jairus	38, 39
A	James, son of Zebedee	13, 33, 62, 78, 79, 90, 104, 118, 120
A	James, son of Alphaeus	33, 120
A	John, son of Zebedee	13, 33, 62, 64, 78, 79, 90, 97, 104, 106, 112, 115, 118, 119, 120
	John the Baptist	4, 8, 9, 10, 11, 15, 16, 20, 39, 40, 45, 57, 76, 85
	Joseph, husband to Mary	4-8, 12
A	Joseph of Arimathea	113, 114
A	Judas, son of James (Thaddaeus)	33, 100, 120
	Judas Iscariot	33, 49, 83, 94, 97, 98, 104, 105, 107, 108
	Lazarus, brother of Mary and Martha	81-83
	Lazarus (parable)	76
	'Legion'	37, 38
	Lysanias, tetrarch of Abilene	9
	Magi	6-7
	Martha (Bethany)	71, 81, 82, 83
	Mary, mother of Jesus	2-8, 13, 31, 112, 120
	Mary Magdalene	43, 112-116
	Mary, mother of James	112, 113
	Mary (Bethany)	71, 81-83
	Mary, wife of Clopas	112, 113
A	Matthew Levi	22, 33, 120

	Moses	15, 21, 47, 50, 55, 58, 62, 68, 76, 77, 116
(A)	Nathaniel (Bartholomew)	12, 33, 118, 120
	Nicodemus	14, 15, 51, 114
A	Philip	12, 33, 46, 94, 99, 120
	Philip, tetrarch of Iturea and Trachonitis	9, 20
	Pilate	9, 107-111, 113, 114
	Quirinius, Governor of Syria	5
	Salome, daughter of Herodias	45
	Salome, disciple of Jesus	112, 114
	Simeon	6
A	Simon Peter	11-13, 33, 47, 49, 61, 62, 64, 66, 69, 73, 90, 97-99, 104-107, 115, 117-120
	Simon of Cyrene	111
	Simon the leper	83
	Simon the Pharisee	42, 43
A	Simon the Zealot	33, 120
A	Thomas	33, 81, 99, 117, 118, 120
	Tiberius, Roman Emperor	9
	Zacchaeus	80
	Zebedee	13
	Zebedee (sons: James, John)	78, 79
	Zebedee's wife	79
	Zechariah	1-4
	Jesus' (?half) brothers: James, Joseph, Simon and Judas	20, 32, 49, 120

SUPPLEMENTARY NOTES INDEX

It is advisable to look at these notes and maps before starting on the gospels, especially those marked # below. The others contain snippets of relevant geographical and historical interest with special reference to The Temple.

#	(i)	The Gospel Writers
#	(ii)	Glossary
#	(iii)	Glossary – continued
#	(iv)	Glossary – continued
#	(v)	MAP – the Roman Empire AD50
	(vi)	Rulers of Palestine
	(vii)	Rulers of Palestine – continued
	(viii)	Moses and the Tabernacle
	(ix)	Moses and the Tabernacle – continued
	(x)	Moses and the Tabernacle – continued
	(xi)	Solomon's Temple
	(xii)	Solomon's Temple – continued
	(xiii)	Solomons Temple – continued
	(xiv)	The Second Temple
#	(xv)	MAP – from Egypt to Chaldea
	(xvi)	The Second Temple – continued
#	(xvii)	MAP – Palestine in New Testament Times
	(xviii)	Pronunciation of Place Names
	(xix)	Jerusalem in New Testament Times
#	(xx)	MAP – Jerusalem in New Testament Times
	(xxi)	Jerusalem in New Testament Times continued
	(xxii)	Temple Mount
	(xxiii)	Temple Mount continued
#	(xxiv)	PLAN – Temple Mount
	(xxv)	Herod's Temple
	(xxvi)	Herod's Temple – continued
	(xxvii)	Herod's Temple – continued
#	(xxviii)	PLAN – Herod's Temple
	(xxix)	Herod's Temple – key to plan opposite
	(xxx)	Temples and Churches – Summary and Conclusion
	(xxxi)	Temples and Churches – Summary and Conclusion – continued
	(xxxii)	Temples and Churches – Summary and Conclusion – continued
#	(xxxiii)	Jewish Religious Feasts
#	(xxxiv)	Jewish Religious Feasts – continued
#	(xxxv)	Jewish Religious Feasts – continued
#	(xxxvi)	The Line of Descent
#	(xxxvii)	The Line of Descent – continued
#	(xxxviii)	The Ancient Prophecies

An introduction to the Gospels according to SS Matthew, Mark, Luke and John

THE GOSPEL WRITERS

MATTHEW – was Jewish. He may have been the apostle whom Jesus called from his desk in the customs office. Dr Moffatt thinks that perhaps he was a teacher. He shows how the events in Jesus' life fulfilled the ancient prophecies to the Jews, and the purpose of God. He used Mark's MS which he sometimes rearranged, or even altered – having access to more material than Mark.

MARK – probably the John Mark mentioned in the Acts of the Apostles. His was the first gospel to be written – in about 65 AD – possibly based on Peter's account of events. A short, vivid history of Jesus' ministry. At the end he breaks off in the middle of a sentence. Was he somehow prevented from finishing his work? – was part of the MS later damaged or lost?

LUKE – a friend of Paul's – not Jewish by birth. He was a doctor, which may explain why it is only Luke who tells us the circumstances of the virgin birth, and Paul never mentions it. Perhaps, in those days, this would be regarded as a delicate subject which a Jew, who must have known Mary, would feel should be left to a physician to describe. Luke may have been the man in Paul's vision who said, 'Come over to Macedonia and help us!' His gospel is addressed to Theophilus – as is the Acts of the Apostles, a sequel to his gospel. Theophilus was perhaps a man of rank – a patron? – a convert to the New Way? Luke, too, had access to Mark's gospel.

see
Appendix

JOHN – the 'disciple whom Jesus loved.' (see John 21:20 p. 119). Jesus called him and his brother, James: 'Boanerges' = Sons of Thunder! His gospel was written at Ephesus towards the end of the first century, perhaps as early as 70 AD. It shows a deep, mystical understanding of Jesus' creation of the world; and he shows that eternal life is to do with the present relationship of the soul with Jesus Christ.

All the gospels were written in Hellenistic Greek. There is no punctuation – not even spaces – just a continuous flow of capital letters! Hellenistic Greek was understood far and wide throughout the Roman Empire.

It is thought that the first written records of Jesus' ministry were in existence by about 50 AD.

GLOSSARY

Example Page

L 6:12   33 APOSTLE – one sent forth – especially with a message.

M 5:4   23 COMFORT – much more than sympathy and consolation, it means
(AV)   also: encouragement, support and strengthening.

L 3:2   9 DESERT WILDERNESS – in Hebrew: "midbar"; not always barren,
           sandy, wasteland; sometimes has scrub, wild trees and grass –
           used for grazing sheep and cattle.

M 4:1   10 DEVIL – from 'diabolos' (Gk) = accuser. 'He accuses us before God
           both day and night.' Revelation 12:10.
           – most wicked angel; implacable enemy and tempter of the human
           race, especially believers, whom he seeks to devour. 'Abaddon'
           (Hebrew); 'Apollyon' (Gk) = destroyer; 'Prince of Darkness'; 'Prince
           of this world' 'Beelzebub' 'Lucifer' etc.

J 2:2   13 DISCIPLE – follower of any leader of thought.

J 21:7 106 NAKED – a man wearing only his tunic was said to be naked, or
(AV)   stripped. Men were sometimes dressed in this way while working –
Mk 14:51 e.g. fishermen.

M 3:7   9 PHARISEES – a widespread religious and political sect thought to
           have originated among devout Jews in the 2nd century BC. Their
           name comes from a Hebrew word meaning Division or Separate;
           they held themselves aloof from others, practising a stricter form of
           religious observance. In their efforts to implement every detail of
           the written Law, as interpreted by the Scribes, they added invented
           traditions of their own and insisted that these also should be
           strictly kept. Gradually the Law and its 'traditions' became a heavy
           burden of trifling, even superstitious, rites and customs, while its
           heart and spirit were neglected. Jesus often reproved them for
           their hypocrisy. But there were many good Pharisees – Nicodemus,
           for one; and they were not all, like the Sadduces, rich and powerful.
(AV)

M 4:5   10 PINNACLE OF THE TEMPLE — according to Josephus the south-east
maps   corner of the battlements of Temple Mount was so high that no one
(xxi)(xxiv) could look down from it to the ravine below without feeling dizzy.

J 1:38 11 RABBI – teacher, master. RABBONI, RABBUNI – my master. J 20:17
(AV)   p.115.

L 24:21 116 REDEEM – to re-purchase something in pawn; to rescue a prisoner in
(AV)   enemy hands; to deliver from guilt and the power of sin – as

wrought by Christ's atonement; to purchase the freedom of another by the payment of ransom.

M 3:7   9 SADDUCES – disciples of Sadoc (Zadoc), who was High Priest in the time of David. They came mostly from rich and powerful Jewish families. Rejecting the traditions of the elders, they held that only the laws written in the Pentateuch (-uke) – the first five books of the Old Testament – particularly those concerning Temple worship, were solemnly binding. Most of the chief priests were Sadduces. They believed in souls, but thought that they were mortal, and in consequence that there was no punishment or reward after death.

L 2:30   6 SALVATION – rescue from danger; rescue from sin – through faith, (AV)   repentance and obedience; the eternal joy hereafter.

M 5:20   23 SCRIBES – were originally stewards in control of the people's access (AV)   to the throne rooms of David and Solomon, over 1000 BC. By about 400 BC they had achieved a position of authority as preservers, teachers and administrators of the Law to the people. Thus it was that the disciples said to Jesus, "Why do *the Scribes* say that first Elijah must come?" And it was the Scribes who challenged Jesus' authority: *"Who gave you the authority?"* – believing that no one but themselves had this right. By the time Jesus was born, they had come to abuse their trust very badly, delivering traditions instead of the Scriptures, which eventually took precedence over the Law itself. When they demanded of Jesus, "Why do your disciples disobey the traditions of the elders?" he swiftly replied, "Why do you disobey the commands of God in your traditions?"

Scribes were not paid for their services and had to earn their livings in various other ways: some were Sadduces, some ordinary priests, and others were artisans and labourers. Many were in the Sanhedrin – the highest legal and administrative body in the

para 3   Jewish state. Gamaliel was one of these, Nicodemus another. The (xx)   Jewish historian, Josephus, was a Scribe.

L 1:77   4 SIN – any thought, word, action, omission or desire contrary to the Law of God. Anything which we allow to stand between us and God – or which does not measure up to his standards – i.e. anything dishonest, impure, selfish or unloving.

(Moffatt)
L 2:7   5 STABLE, STALL – "Mary wrapped the baby Jesus in swaddling clothes
L 13:15   and laid him in a stall." In most versions the Greek word for 'stall' is translated as 'manger.' The dictionary definition of 'stall' is: 'a single compartment for the use of one animal in a cow-house, stable, etc.'

Example Page

L 2:7
(AV)

⁵SWADDLING or SWATHING BANDS – in the time of Jesus these were used by a good mother to wrap her babies for the first six months of their lives. This was thought to help the infants' arms and legs to grow straight and strong – it was a mark of parental care.

Jesus would have been bathed, rubbed all over with salt to guard against infection, and then wrapped in a piece of cloth. This was folded over at his feet and sides, and all secured with bands – strips of material, often embroidered. Perhaps once or twice a day the baby was removed from his wrappings and washed, gently rubbed with olive oil or dusted with powdered, dried myrtle leaves – and re-wrapped. Swathing bands are still used in remote rural areas in the Middle East and in Russia.

L 15:8

(AV)

⁶⁵TEN PIECES OF SILVER – Jesus may have been referring to the coins of a bridal headband, often worn to display the bride's dowry.

L 3:1

⁹TETRARCH – tetra is a Greek word meaning 'four'. In the Roman Empire a tetrarch was the governor of a fourth part of a country or province; a subordinate ruler. 'Ethnarch' = the ruler of the largest fourth.

M 19:24

⁶⁹THE EYE OF THE NEEDLE – may have been the name of a pedestrians' gate in the city wall.

L 3:2

⁹WILDERNESS, DESERT – in Hebrew 'midbar'; not always barren, sandy wasteland – sometimes had scrub, wild trees and grass, used for grazing sheep and cattle.

M 4.15
Isa. 9:1

²⁰ZEBULUN and NAPHTALI – two of the twelve tribes of Israel, whose territory was in the land of Galilee.

G □= *see reference to this Glossary*

Note: the symbols « » are used instead of inverted commas for words spoken by God.

The words in brackets ( ) are supplementary to the text.

THE ROMAN EMPIRE AD50

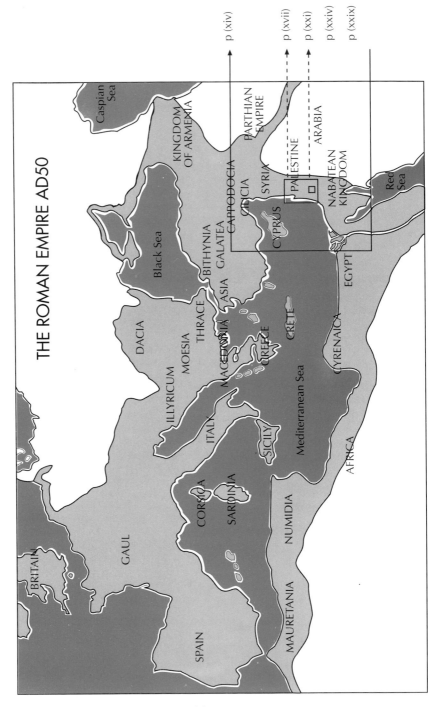

p (xiv)

p (xvii)

p (xxi)

p (xxiv)

p (xxix)

THE RULERS OF PALESTINE

Because of its geographical situation, Palestine was a strategic prize to whoever could control it.

Down the centuries before Jesus was born it was invaded and ruled by Assyrians, Babylonians, Persians, the Ptolemies (Egypt – 301 BC) and, finally, the Seleucids (Syria – 198 BC).

In 164 BC Judas Maccabeus led a revolt in Judea and recaptured the Temple. (See Feast of Dedication p. xxxv). In 142 BC a treaty was signed with Antioch and Simon, Judas' brother, was made High Priest and General Ruler of the Jews. That was the beginning of the Hasmonean Dynasty – named after the tribal surname of Judas Maccabeus.

But vice, intrigue and cruelty grew into monstrous and brutal in-fighting until the death of King Janneus in 76 BC. His wife, Salome Alexandra, then ruled peacefully for nine years; but when she died her two sons fought over the succession and civil war broke out. The two sons appealed to Rome for help and the Roman General, Pompey, readily stepped in. He stormed Jerusalem and put one of the sons, Hyrcanus II, on the throne as High Priest and Subject Prince – but curtailed his power and his territory.

page (xvii)

Hyrcanus' principal adviser was Antipater, the governor of Idumea. He managed to ingratiate himself with Julius Caesar, who had just returned to a hero's welcome in Rome after his famous conquests in Gaul, and had taken over the government from, the now ageing, Pompey. Antipater was promoted to Chief Minister of all Judea, and he made his son, Herod, Governor of Galilee. Herod kept on the right side of Rome and, with their help, he finally secured the throne in 37 BC. He was known as Herod the Great.

G

When Herod died – at the time when the angel, Gabriel, told Joseph that he could bring Mary and the infant Jesus home from Egypt – Israel was divided into four provinces (tetrarchies). Archelaus, Herod's eldest son, was made Governor of Judea. The rest was divided between two other sons (Herod Philip and Herod Antipas) and Lysanias. But Archelaus lacked his father's ability to control and balance the opposing factions in Judea and his ethnarchy soon erupted in revolt. The Roman Governor of Syria had to come in with a large army to quell the revolt; and the Emperor, Augustus, declared Archelaus' inheritance. 'an official province of Rome.' It was thereafter ruled by a succession of

military prefects, the most famous of whom was Pontius Pilate –
about 25 years later – when –

L 3:1   ". . . the word came to John, son of Zechariah, in the desert . . .
page (xvii)   Tiberius was in his fifteenth year as Emperor, Pontius Pilate was
Governor of Judea, Herod Antipas was Tetrarch of Galilee and
Perea, Herod Philip, his brother, was Tetrarch of Iturea and
Trachonitis, and Lysanias was Tetrarch of Abilene."

ROMAN EMPERORS IN NEW TESTAMENT TIMES

Augustus	43 BC – 14 AD	Claudius	41 AD – 54 AD
Tiberius	14 AD – 37 AD	Nero	54 AD – 68 AD
Caligula	37 AD – 41 AD	Vespasian	69 AD – 79 AD

MOSES AND THE TABERNACLE

The Jews were a nomadic race until about 960 BC when King Solomon built the first Temple in Jerusalem (see also p. (xxxiv) – Tabernacles and Tents).

About
1270 BC

THE TABERNACLE

– was a movable temple constructed by the Jews under the direction of Moses, who was given precise instructions by God as to its measurements, building materials, furnishings and the ritual ceremonies which were to take place in it.

Ex. 38.9-13
J 67

Moses first made an open court, 75' x 150', and in its centre was placed the Tabernacle, with its front to the east – "so that the rising sun might send its first rays upon it."

Its interior was protected against sun and rain by curtains of fine twisted linen which were spread over the top of the structure. These were overlaid with slightly larger curtains made of finest white goats hair, and, over all, were layers of curtains made of skins.

THE HOLY OF HOLIES, THE INNER SHRINE OR MOST HOLY PLACE

– formed the western end of the Tabernacle. It was about 15' square, and was partitioned from the rest of the Tabernacle – the Holy Place or Sanctuary – by four gold-plated pillars hung with veils of finest linen. The first, which had purple, blue and scarlet

*see Kherubs
p. (ix)

colours, of 'cunning work with cherubim*,' was 15' square and concealed the Most Holy Place. Josephus says that 'the priests crept under it.' The shrine had no windows and was in complete darkness. It contained:

The Ark of the Covenant

This was a beautiful box, 4' x 2½' x 2½' (high), made of very hard acacia wood and completely covered with gold inside and out. Some say that it was made in the shape of a building rather than box-shaped. It had four gold rings for its carrying poles. Inside it were placed:

J 69
Heb 8&9
esp. 9:4

The Two Sacred Tablets whereupon the Ten Commandments were written – 'five on each tablet, two and a half on each side'; a golden pot of manna; and Aaron's rod – 'that once blossomed.'

The cover was made of pure gold; and two golden* kherubs p (ix) were made, of a piece with the cover, one at each end, facing each other – their outspread wings overshadowing the Ark, to denote the protection of God. This cover was called:

The Mercy Seat

Ex. 25:
17-22

In the space above it would rest the most gracious presence of God.

J 69   *Kherubs* – are 'flying creatures; but their form is not like to that of any of the creatures that men have seen, though Moses said that he had seen such beings near the throne of God.' (The same as 'cherub' (s) 'cherubim' (pl)).

The Jews sometimes took the Ark into battle, when the knowledge of its presence would strengthen their flagging confidence and determination and undermine the morale of the enemy. It was once captured by the Philistines, but they soon became extremely anxious to return it to Israel. Chapter 5 of the first book of Samuel tells why; and chapter 4 describes the battle in which it was lost.

THE HOLY PLACE OR SANCTUARY – was furnished with –

J 69   *The golden table for the shewbread*
This was placed on the north side of the Sanctuary. Upon it twelve loaves, one for each of the tribes of Israel, were arranged in two heaps, with two vials of frankincense set, one upon the top of each.

Ex. 25:32   *The golden, seven-branched candlestick* – a menorah
Also made of pure gold, this candlestick stood opposite to the table, on the south side. It was placed obliquely – "the seven lamps looked to the east and to the south."

The altar of incense
Covered with gold – even the raised grate upon it, which was also surrounded by a crown of gold. It stood $1^{1}/_{2}$' square x 3' high between the candlestick and the table, in front of the Holy of Holies.

A BRAZEN ALTAR – MADE OF ACACIA WOOD AND OVERLAID WITH BRONZE – stood in the court outside the Tabernacle. It was for burnt offerings. The hearth was of bronze network – "the ashes fell through to the ground." Exodus 27:3 speaks of "his pans to receive his ashes" (A.V.) which were no doubt set on the ground under the hearth. It was $7^{1}/_{2}$' square x $4^{1}/_{2}$' high.

J 69   Beside this altar were "basons, vials, censers and cauldrons, all of gold."

Ex. 40:7   Between the brazen altar and the Tabernacle was placed:

The Laver
This was a huge basin of bronze, set upon a bronze base. Filled with water, it was used for washing the hands and feet of the priests before and after the sacrifices were made.

PASSAGES REFERRING TO THE TABERNACLE AND THE ARK OF THE COVENANT

Exodus 24-30 and 35-40
2 Samuel 6-7 (How David brought the Ark of the Covenant to Jerusalem)
Josephus 'Antiquities of the Jews' pages 67-69

About
1200 BC
J 113

NOTE, ACCORDING TO JOSEPHUS, ON THE DEATH OF MOSES

When Moses was about to die, "men, women and children fell into tears". Moses himself – "although he was always persuaded that he ought not to be cast down at the approach of death, since the undergoing of it was agreeable to the will of God, and the law of nature, yet what the people did overbore him that he wept himself."

He lived to 120 and did not die – "although he wrote in the holy books that he died, which was done out of fear lest they should venture to say that because of his extraordinary virtue he went to God."

On Mount Abarim (near Jericho) – "he dismissed the senate and, as he was going to embrace Eleazar and Joshua, and was still discoursing with them, a cloud stood over him on the sudden and he disappeared."

SOLOMON'S TEMPLE

About
1000 BC
2 Sam
24:18
1 Chron
21:18-28

DAVID

At God's behest King David bought Ornan's threshing floor on Mount Moriah in Jerusalem for 1,000 golden guineas, and built there an altar for the Lord.

David spoke to Solomon, his son, of his own longing to build a Temple to the Lord, of the prevention of this by God and the command to charge Solomon with the task. Then David, aware of his son's youth and inexperience, decided that he himself must make arrangements in advance – "so David made ample preparations before he died."

2 Chron
2:16

He gave careful instructions to Solomon and collected in readiness vast amounts of gold, silver, bronze and iron – also timber from Tyre and Sidon, felled in Lebanon under the command of Hiram, King of Tyre, "and forwarded in floats, by sea, to Joppa," and he ordered all the authorities to help Solomon. Thousands of priestly experts were registered to assist and superintend the work.

"So when David was old and full of days, he made Solomon, his son, king over Israel." Further preparations were made, including the making of musical instruments.

David assembled all the authorities in Jerusalem, and he gave to Solomon most detailed plans for the building, the vessels to be used, golden lampstands, tables, implements, the altar of incense –

*p. (ix)

even for the great golden kherubs* which were to stand with their enormous wings outstretched over the Ark of the Covenant. He said to Solomon, "All these plans I have been inspired to write down by the Lord who has instructed me . . . and at every turn you will be supported by every willing and expert workman in every department. Besides this, the authorities and the whole of the nation will be entirely at your command."

He addressed the entire assembly, pledging his own private treasure "to the Temple of my God." The heads of clans and families made freewill offerings, and David gave thanks and praise to the Lord. He prayed for God's direction of the hearts and minds of the people building the Temple.

The people blessed the Lord and made sacrifices and thank-offerings; and they crowned Solomon king for the second time.

Approx
965 BC
2 Chron 1:1

SOLOMON

"King David, the son of Jesse, died in a good old age, full of days, riches and honour; and Solomon, his son, reigned in his stead." (end of 1 Chron)

J 219

Solomon wrote to Hiram, his and his father's friend, as follows:

"My father would have built a Temple to God, but was hindered by wars and continual expeditions . . . for God foretold to my father that such an house should be built by me . . ." King Hiram provided more timber, and one of his finest master craftsmen, also called Hiram, who was expert in precious metalwork, bronze, iron, stone and wood, the treatment and dyeing of linen, and carving and engraving of all kinds.

Solomon began the building . . . "the foundations were very deep." "The sound of no hammer or any other tool of iron was heard while the Temple was being built." There were 80,000 stone masons at work in the hills.

The foundations were 90' x 30' and the porch 15' x 30'. The main body of the Temple was 45' high.

THE HOLY OF HOLIES

This Inner Shrine was now 30' square and 30' high, and it contained the Ark of the Covenant resting on its stand with its carrying poles at rest in their rings, as in the time of Moses.

Then Solomon made the two magnificent kherubs, to his father's design. Before gilding they were carved from olive wood and they stood 15' tall, their outspread wings spanning 15'. Their wingtips met above the Ark, while their other wings touched the walls on either side; and their faces were turned towards the Ark. At this time the Ark contained only the two sacred stone tablets of the Ten Commandments.

The walls of the Holy of Holies were carved with cherubim and palm trees and open flowers; and everything in the shrine, even the floor, was overlaid with gold. It was, as always, in complete darkness.

Then Solomon built side rooms against the outside walls of the sides and the western end of the Temple. Some were used for storing gold, and the Temple implements and vessels which were made of precious metals.

There were three altars in Solomon's Temple. A great altar, for burnt offerings, was built in the outer court at the east end of the Temple structure, because the bronze altar, 30' square and 15' high was not able to hold the burnt offering, the cereal offering and the fat slices. The third was the altar of incense – made of gold by Solomon himself. He also made all the golden utensils used in the Temple as well as the cast, bright bronze work.

The golden, seven-branched candlestick was also present in the Holy Place.

King Hiram's master craftsman made a vast amount of bronze work, besides the bronze altar, including:

1 Kings 7:23	a new laver – a large metal 'sea', or pool, 15' across and 7½' deep. This was set upon the backs of twelve brazen bulls, three facing to each point of the compass, sitting on their haunches, the better to take the weight of the pool and the water, in it ten bronze water trolleys, wonderfully decorated, each with its 320-gallon bronze pot many implements including shovels, bowls etc.
Jer 52: 20-23 2 Chron 3:15 1 Kings 7:15	two huge bronze columns for the vestibule of the Temple. These were 27' high, 18' in circumference (6' in diameter), with capitals 7½' high. They were made of 3" thick plates of bronze and were hollow. He even gave them names – 'Jachin' on the right, and 'Boaz' on the left.
Jer 52 2 Kings 25	Solomon started to build the Temple in 960 BC and it stood until 587 BC when it was destroyed by Nebuchadnezzar II of Babylonia (Chaldea). The Temple was burnt as well as the palace and the houses in Jerusalem; the soldiers tore down the city walls and the Temple treasures were removed to Babylon. Nearly all the Jews were taken into captivity.

NOTE

2 Chron 4:10 "The tank, or sea, was placed at the right side of the Temple facing south-east."

1 Kings 7:39 "The tank was placed on the south side of the Temple at the eastern corner."

(Therefore 'right' and 'left' meant: as one stood with one's back to the Holy of Holies – looking east – NOT as if one were standing at the door of the Temple, looking in).

THE SECOND TEMPLE

Isa 44:28
Isa 45
In the 7th century BC Isaiah prophesied: "(The Lord says) « I am he who says to Cyrus ‹ He is my friend, he executes my purposes › » Thus the Lord, the true God, hails Cyrus, whom he consecrates – « whose right hand I have grasped, to terrify the nations . . . It is I who have raised Cyrus of set purpose, smoothing the path for him; it is he who shall rebuild my city and set free my exiles »"

Jer 25:11
Jer 29:10
In the 6th century the prophet Jeremiah predicted that the Lord would restore the Jews to their homeland within 70 years.

2 Chron 36:22
Ezra 1
J 300
In 586 BC the Jews were taken into captivity, and in 539 BC Cyrus the Great of Persia conquered Babylon. A year later, after reading Isaiah's prophecy about his role in history, Cyrus "was seized with an earnest desire and ambition to fulfil it". He set about sending the Jews back to Israel, returning the Temple's precious treasures which had been locked away in the Babylonian palace vaults; and he gave a great deal of financial and other, practical support towards their efforts to rebuild the Temple.

Haggai 2:3
Ezra 3:12
J 300
Work began at once, but the Jews became discouraged and their efforts flagged. The prophets Haggai and Zechariah spurred them on and it was finally finished in 515 BC. But, at the celebrations of the completion of the Second Temple, the sounds of joyful chanting and music were at times drowned by the lamentations of those Jews who were old enough to remember the grandeur of Solomon's Temple, which far surpassed its replacement.

Although there is a long inventory of the Temple treasures which were brought back from Babylon, there is no word of the Ark of the Covenant and its most precious contents, or about the great golden kherubs . . .

Jer 3:14
Before the captivity, Jeremiah had prophesied: "The Lord said to me, « Turn again, O backsliding children! – for it is I who am your Lord. I will take one or two of you, one from a town here, two from a clan there, and bring you to Sion where I will give you rulers after my own heart who shall furnish you with knowledge and with sense. In after days, when you become numerous and fruitful in the land, men shall no longer speak of 'The Ark of the Covenant'. That shall never enter their minds; they shall not remember it, they shall never miss it, and it shall never be remade. They shall

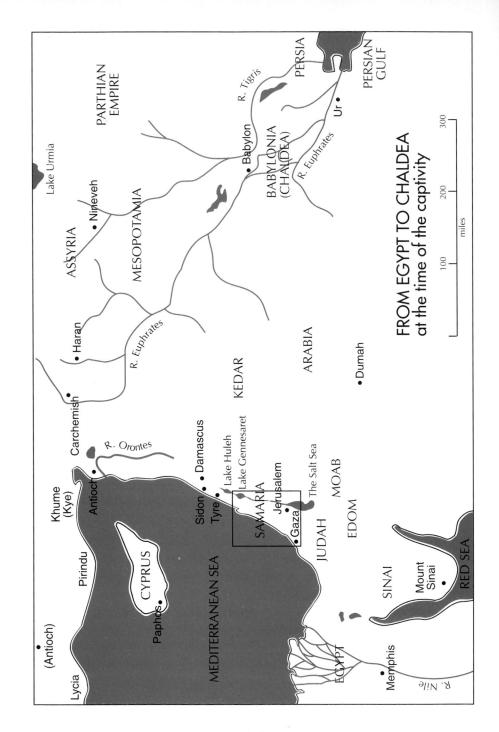

FROM EGYPT TO CHALDEA
at the time of the captivity

miles

| 100 | 200 | 300 |

(xv)

call Jerusalem, then, 'the throne of the Lord,' and all nations shall gather to it, living no longer by the stubbornness of their evil minds »"

Heb 9:3
Rev 11:19 This is the last time the Ark of the Covenant is mentioned – except for Paul's reference to it in his letter to the Hebrews, and, in the Revelation of St. John, the words: "Then the Temple of God in heaven was thrown open and the Ark of the Covenant was seen inside his Temple."

From the time of the captivity, the Holy of Holies remained empty of everything except "the most gracious presence of God."

The Second Temple stood from 515 BC until 20 BC, when it was demolished by Herod preparatory to rebuilding it.

PALESTINE IN NEW TESTAMENT TIMES
showing the places mentioned in the four gospels

*Emmaus Nicopolis Emmaus Colonia Amasa
– the latter likely to be mentioned in Luke 24

(xvii)

PRONUNCIATION OF PLACE NAMES

Abilene	Ab i LEEN ee	Jerusalem	Jer OO sal em
Aenon	EE non	Judea	Joo DEE uh
Arimathea	Arrim ath EE uh	Magadan*	MAG uh dan
Bethabara	Beth AB bar uh	Masada	Mass AH duh
Bethany	BETH an i	Nabatea	Nab a TEE uh
Bethlehem	BETH li hem	Nain	NANE
Bethphage	Beth FAH gay	Naphtali†	NAF tuh lie
Bethsaida	Beth SAY i duh	Nazareth	NAZ uh reth
Cana	CANE uh	Perea	Peh REE uh
Capernaum	Cap UR nay um	Phoenicia	Foe NEE shi uh
Chorazin	Caw RAY zin	Rama	RAH muh
Damascus	Da MASS cus	Samaria	Sam AIR i uh
Decapolis	De CAP oh liss	Sarepta	Suh REP tuh
Emmaus	Em MAY us	Sidon	SIGH dn
Ephraim	EE fray im	Sychar	SIGH car
Gadara	GAD ah ruh	Tiberias	Ty BEE ree uhs
Galilee	GAL i lee	Trachonitis	Track on IGH tis
Gaza	GAH zuh	Tyre	TIRE
Gennesaret	Geh NESS ah ret	Tyropoeon	Tie ROE pian
Idumea	Id yoo MEE uh	Zebulun†	ZEBB yoo lun
Iturea	It yoo REE uh		
Jericho	JERR i coe	†see page (iv)	

NOTE

The Sea of Galilee was also called Lake Gennesaret and Lake Tiberias.

*Magadan was also known as Magdala (MAG duh luh). It was either the birthplace or the home of Mary Magdalene.

Mark, in 8·10, refers to Dalmanutha (Dul muh NEW thuh). This could be close to, or another name for, Magadan (M 15:39).

JERUSALEM IN NEW TESTAMENT TIMES

p. (vi)
p.(xvii)

Herod the Great was King of Judea from 37 BC - 4 BC. He was Idumean by birth but he adopted the Jewish religion. He embarked upon a vast building programme throughout Israel which involved wonderful feats of engineering skill, including two new cities, one of which was the great sea port of Caesarea Maritima. He also built many luxurious palaces, public buildings and monuments.

He transformed Jerusalem into one of the most brilliant of the Roman provincial cities in the east, building a hippodrome, an amphitheatre, a theatre, baths and many other public buildings. The Temple was reconstructed on a gigantic scale in an enlarged precinct which overhung the Tyropoeon (Cheesemaker's) Valley on the west and the Kidron Ravine on the east, 'on retaining walls of incomparable workmanship and dizzy height.'

p. (xxi)
p. (xxiv)

He also converted the old Maccabean castle, or 'Baris', into a fortified residence for himself which he named the Antonia Tower to gratify his friend Anthony; and he built another, much larger, royal palace on the western hill, with three giant towers for its defence set into the adjoining city wall. The writers of the Oxford Bible Atlas have concluded that this palace is identical with Pilate's Praetorium and that 'the Pavement' (Gabbatha) mentioned in John 19:13 was probably an open, paved space on the western hill, perhaps just inside the Gennath Gate. The famous stone pavement still accessible on the site of the Antonia Tower, with a Roman triple arch, popularly known as the Ecce Homo Arch, belonged to the central court of the Antonia Tower, and the arch itself to the Roman city of Aelia Capitolina, which was not built until the 1st or 2nd century AD.

In AD 66 a succession of ill-advised and corrupt Roman Governors turned a simmering anti-Roman resentment into violent resistance. Jewish protests against an act of deliberate sacrilege by some Greeks, met with an insensitive and brutal response: the Roman Governor arrested the Jews and plundered the Temple treasury. When the Jews protested again he sent troops into Jerusalem and, in the ensuing slaughter, more than three thousand men, women and children were killed. There was immediate open rebellion. The Jews attacked the Romans with such anger and ferocity that they drove them out of Jerusalem and

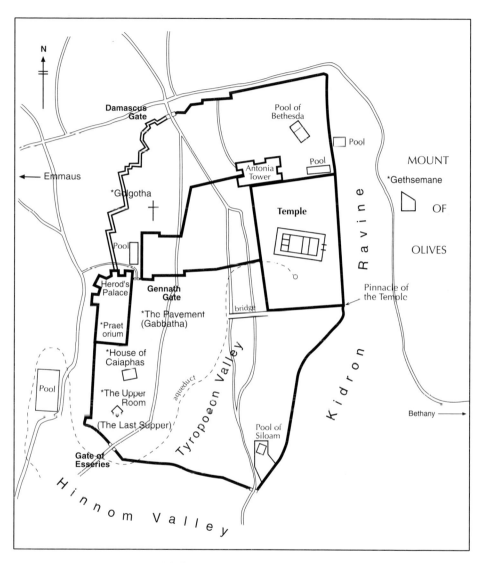

JERUSALEM IN NEW TESTAMENT TIMES

*traditional or conjectural

SCALE: The east wall of Temple Mount is 500 yards long

═══ Wall of Aelia

Aelia Capitolina was a Roman colony planted by Hadrian in AD 130 on the site of Jerusalem which had been destroyed AD70

(xx)

p. 84
L 19:41-44
p. 90
M 24:1
p. 92
L 21:22
recaptured two fortresses. But then the Roman Emperor, Nero, sent in three Roman legions commanded by Vespasian (later to succeed Nero as Emperor). They marched through Galilee and soon occupied all of Palestine except for Jerusalem and three fortresses. Jerusalem fell in AD 70 and the Temple was reduced to rubble just as Jesus had prophesied. The following year Vespasian staged a triumphal march through the streets of Rome, with high-ranking Jewish captives and treasures looted from the Temple.

map
p. (xvii)
It was three more years before the Romans occupied the last of the fortresses, Masada. This was an almost impregnable stronghold and the rebels defended it with the grim courage of desperation. When the Romans finally smashed and burned their way into its centre they found that all the Jews there, nearly a thousand men, women and children, had committed suicide rather than submit to their enemies.

When the Roman legions marched through Galilee in AD 68 they captured Joseph ben Matthias, General of the Jewish forces in Galilee. After his surrender Joseph, with great presence of mind, predicted that Vespasian would become Emperor; and when this prediction came true his future was assured. He adopted the Emperor's family name, Flavius, and was granted the rights of a Roman citizen. After the war he lived in Rome and wrote a history of the Jews − from the Creation to the fall of Masada. He was known as *Flavius Josephus.*

Archaeological research continually strives to establish the location and the history of the places mentioned in the Bible. There has been much success, but there are still many sites marked 'traditional only.'

For fuller information see: Oxford Bible Atlas
Jesus and His Times

TEMPLE MOUNT

Archeological research on Temple Mount is severely limited because the site is hallowed to Christians, Jews and Muslims alike.

see pp. (xi)-(xiv)

The first Temple was built in Jerusalem by King Solomon nearly 1,000 years BC. In 586 BC it was destroyed by the Babylonians under Nebuchadnezzar II, when thousands of Jews were taken in chains to Babylon.

About fifty years later, Cyrus the Great of Persia conquered Babylon, and in the first year of his reign he set about returning the Jews to Israel and helped them to begin rebuilding the Temple. It was finally completed in 515 BC and stood until 20 BC when it was demolished by Herod preparatory to rebuilding it.

Herod's Temple was truly magnificent. Built on a much larger scale than the previous Temples, its precincts – the Temple Mount – covered about 30 acres.

maps pp. (xxi) (xxiv)

The east wall of the Mount overhung the Kidron ravine. To support it, and the cloister to be built against it, Herod first strengthened the rocks below, binding them together with lead and "fastening their inner parts with iron" to make a foundation as strong as the hill itself. He increased the height of the foundation to bring it level with the rest of the Mount, smoothed off the top and outer surfaces and built the wall and the double cloister along its edge. This cloister faced the east gate of the Temple enclosure.

The four gates in the west wall of Temple Mount led:

1. via a passage over the Tyropoeon (Cheesemakers') Valley, to Herod's palace.
2. \
3. / to the city suburbs.
4. to the 'other city' – with a great number of steps down into the valley and up the other side.

In the south wall there was a central gate, and from the east wall to the west were the triple, Royal Cloisters. The wall below was so deep that 'you could not see to the bottom of it and, with the height of the cloister itself, to look down from the top of the battlements there was dizzying to any man.'

The gate in the east wall, known as the Golden Gate, led across a viaduct to the Mount of Olives (Olivet).

The first enclosure – the Court of the Gentiles – was open to all – even to non-Jews. There were money-changers in the surrounding cloisters or colonnades, and birds and animals were on sale.

The second Temple enclosure, 'to be gone up by a few steps,' was completely encircled by a stone balustrade which bore notices carved in stone, with the letters painted in red, in Latin and Greek: 'No foreigner may enter within the balustrade and enclosure around the Temple. Anyone caught doing so will bear the responsibility for his own ensuing death.'

Precise plans and measurements of the Temple are not known. The map and the plans which follow are based on scraps of information gleaned from the Bible, the works of Josephus and archeological research.

'Antiquities of the Jews' – Flavius Josephus pp. 462-464.

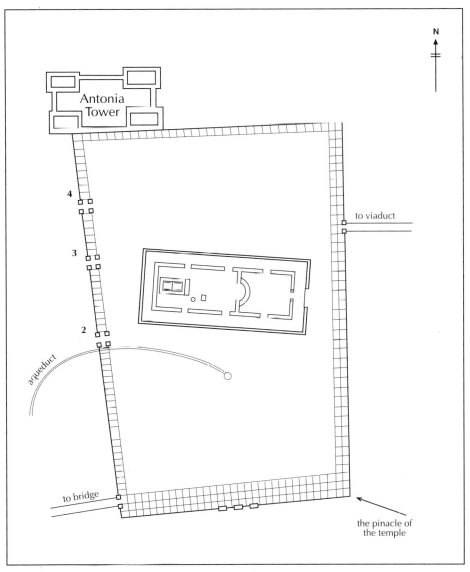

N

Antonia
Tower

4

3

2

aqueduct

to viaduct

to bridge

the pinacle of
the temple

TEMPLE MOUNT

Scale:
The length of the east wall is approx. 500 yards.

HEROD'S TEMPLE

Please refer to the following maps and plans

JERUSALEM IN NEW TESTAMENT TIMES
THE TEMPLE MOUNT
HEROD'S TEMPLE

Precise measurements and plans of Herod's Temple do not exist and this map and the plans are partly conjectural.

THE TEMPLE MOUNT

Against the east wall of the Temple Mount Herod build a double cloister. This wall measured 1,500'.

The north wall, approx. 990', was made in line with the south wall of the Antonia Tower.

The west wall, with its four gates, was cloistered. Approx. 1,530'.

The south wall, approx. 880', besides the gate leading to Herod's palace, had a gate at its centre. Against this wall, from its east end to its west was the Royal Cloister.

'Three walks' ran the length of this cloister – there were four rows of pillars opposite to each other, the fourth being incorporated into the outer wall. There were 162 pillars in all, 27' tall, with a circumference 'such that three men could just link hands around them. They had a double spiral at their base and the 'chapiters' were sculptured in the Corinthian style.' It had three walls, the centre wall rising to a height of 100' and the two others to 50'. The roofs were deeply sculptured with figures of many kinds, and the wall in front was amazingly fine – 'adorned with beams resting on the pillars that were interwoven into it. That front was all of polished stone.'

THE TEMPLE ENCLOSURE

In the middle of this first enclosure, was the second, 'to be gone up by a few steps.' (Encompassed by the stone balustrade).

This second 'enclosure' was a vast building which contained:
- the Court of the Women
- the Court of the Israelites
- the Court of the Priests
- the Temple itself – the Holy of Holies and the Holy Place.

In this building there were three gates, equidistant from each other, on the north and south sides. At the east end was one large gate – possibly the one referred to as 'The Gate Beautiful' – to admit 'the pure and their wives.' This led into the Court of the women, on the opposite side of which was the magnificent Nicanor Gate – approached by a flight of fifteen curved steps. No women were allowed to pass through this gate into the Court of the Israelites and, between this court and the Holy Place and the Most Holy Place, was the Court of the Priests for the priests alone to enter. (Except on the Day of Atonement). Much of this Court was open to the sky, for here stood the great altar for sacrifices and burnt offerings.

Herod was not admitted to any of these courts because he was not a priest. However, he took care of the cloisters and the outer enclosures which took him eight years to build. Herod also built a secret passage from the Antonia Tower to the east gate of the Temple over which he built himself a tower. This subterranean passage was designed 'to guard against sedition.'

THE TEMPLE

The Sanctuary and the Holy of Holies were completed in a year and a half because Herod, like David and Solomon centuries before him, had trained all his artisans, many of them priests, and carefully prepared all the materials before he began. But the Temple courts were not finished until AD 63, long after Herod's death, and only seven years before all the buildings were totally destroyed by the Romans.

The foundations were 150' long and 30' higher than the previous level. Huge white stones were used: $37\frac{1}{2}$' x 12' x 18'.

This central structure was much higher than the surrounding courts and, as with the Royal Cloisters at the south wall, it could be seen from a long way off. The Temple doors and lintel were as high as the Temple itself, and the doors were hung with embroidered veils with purple flowers and pillars interwoven. Over these, from below the crown work, was hung a huge golden vine, its branches hanging down from a great height.

The outside walls of the Temple, and the doors, were covered with gold. It must have been a dazzling sight, especially at sunrise and sunset. It was written in the Talmud: "He who has not seen the Temple of Herod has never seen a beautiful building."

Siderooms were built inside the outer walls of the courts and against the outside of the walls of the Holy of Holies and the Most Holy Place. Among these were:

The Treasury Chambers

– the Shekel Chamber, which held the revenue from the Temple Tax – a half-shekel a year.
– the Utensils Chamber – for the storage of gold and silver vessels which were used in the services.
– the Secrets Chamber, which held funds for "the poor of good family."
– the Safe Keeping Chamber, which held safe deposits.

In the Court of the Women
Special chambers were reserved for:

- lepers – where the priests would inspect people who had recovered from leprosy and pronounce them cured – or not.
- wood – for the storage of wood for the sacrifices. This had to be good, worm-free wood.
- oil and wine – for use in the services.
- the Nazirites – set aside for people who were under special, holy vows.

Also in the Court of Women were the treasury chests, shaped like shofars (ram's horn trumpets) to receive the people's offerings (see Mk 12:41 and L 21:1 p. 90 in this book).

When the building of the Temple was complete there were feasts and general celebrations. Thanks were given to God; and thanks were also given to Herod for his speed in the work of construction. These celebrations were joyfully combined with those for the King's inauguration.

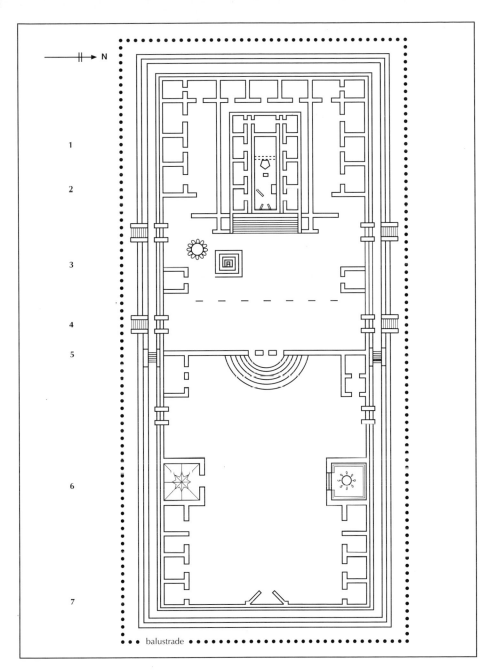

N

1

2

3

4

5

6

7

balustrade

HEROD'S TEMPLE
Key on page (xxix) overleaf

(xxviii)

1. The Holy of Holies – in complete darkness and empty of everything except the gracious presence of God.

2. The Holy Place or Sanctuary
    the seven-branched candlestick of pure gold – a menorah –
    the golden altar of incense
    the golden table for the shewbread
    side rooms – including strong rooms for the Temple treasures, the safe keeping chamber, shekel chamber, chamber of secrets etc.

3. The altar – 30' square x 15' high – possibly a ziggurat – ; the circular pool, or sea, 15' across x 7½' deep, set upon twelve brazen bulls, sitting on their haunches so that they could support the weight of the sea and the water in it. Water trolleys and lavers, golden vessels and implements. The Court of the Priests – open to the sky – for priests only, except on the day of Atonement.

4. The Court of the Israelites – for men only.

5. The magnificent Nicanor Gate – approached by fifteen curved steps.

6. The Court of the Women – open to all Jews.

    The chambers of   lepers
                        wood
                        oil and wine
                        the Nazirites
                        the treasury – with thirteen treasury chests shaped like shofarim (ram's horn trumpets) etc.

7. The entrance to the Temple – massive double doors – probably the 'Gate Beautiful.' Solomon's Porch may also have been at this end of the Temple.

TEMPLES AND CHURCHES – SUMMARY AND CONCLUSION

The Bible tells the history of a nation directed by God. From Genesis onwards we read of kings, leaders, ordinary folk, who heard God's word and obeyed it – such people as Abraham, David, Solomon and the prophets. We can see that when the people listened to God and obeyed his will, marvellous events followed; and whenever they failed to do so – things went painfully wrong. It is the same today.

We can follow the records of places, tents and buildings provided by God as centres where people could meet to worship him – a history which is continuing today.

GENESIS – When God spoke to *Abraham* he listened, and followed the path shown to him. He and his people were led from Ur of the Chaldees to Canaan (see map on p. (xiv)*. Abraham built altars to the Lord and called on his name (Gen. 12:8). There was no priesthood or ritual.

EXODUS – 13TH CENTURY BC – through *Moses,* God led his people from slavery in Egypt to freedom, and made a Holy Covenant with them. He gave them:

– the Ten Commandments, written on tablets of stone, and the Law. These command us to love God with all our might, and our neighbours as ourselves.

– as a focus for the people's worship of him, he gave detailed instructions for the building of an *Ark* in which to keep the tablets of stone; and the *Tabernacle* – and minute details about the form of worship to be observed. Sometimes he even hallowed the Tabernacle with his very Presence.

SAMUEL, CHRONICLES, KINGS, JEREMIAH – 11TH CENTURY BC – God inspired and directed *King David* to make the plans for the first Temple, to be built by his son, Solomon.

ISAIAH, JEREMIAH, CHRONICLES, HAGGAI, EZRA – 6TH CENTURY BC – When the Israelites came to forsake God's ways, and were walking in great danger, God sent them the prophet, *Jeremiah.* But despite Jeremiah's impassioned pleadings, the people refused to listen . . . Nebuchadnezzar II of Babylonia overran Israel, destroyed the Temple, looted its treasures and took most of the Israelites in captivity to Babylon (Chaldea – see * above).

As prophesied by Isaiah and Jeremiah, God used *Cyrus the Great* of Persia as his instrument – to conquer Babylon and help the Israelites to return home and to build a *Second Temple.*

The Ark of the Covenant and its precious contents had been lost. See the prophecy of Jeremiah and the words of John in the book of Revelation (pages (xv) (xvi)).

1ST CENTURY BC – *Herod* replaced the Second Temple with the t*hird,* and most magnificent Temple of all.

THE NEW TESTAMENT

Then the Light came into the world. "God so loved the world that J 3:16 p.15 he gave his only Son so that all who believe in him may not die, but have eternal life." Born (incarnate) by the Holy Spirit of the Virgin Mary, Jesus Christ, the Son of God came to earth in person. It pleased him to call himself "the Son of Man". He reminded the Jews that God requires mercy, not sacrifice; that "the M 9:13 sacrifices of God are . . . a broken and a contrite heart."
Psa. 51:17 He said that God, the loving Creator of all, is a Spirit. His kingdom is not of this world but of the Spirit; therefore, to enter it, J 3:5 p.15 a person has to be born for a second time. Flesh and blood can give birth to flesh and blood, but only Spirit can give birth to Spirit.

He said that "the gate is narrow and the way is hard that leads M 7:13 to Life, and only a few find it." But there it is – wide open to all P.27 who believe in the Son of God and obey his word; and he has promised to be with us every step of the way. All are invited, and J 6:37 no one who comes to Jesus will ever be turned away.

From his childhood he regularly attended synagogue and Temple, following the pattern of worship set by his Father in ancient times.

"Give unto the Lord, ye kindreds of the people; give unto the 1 Chron Lord glory and strength. Give unto the Lord the glory due to his 16:28 name; bring an offering, and come before him. Worship the Lord in the beauty of holiness."

From the time of the Babylonian captivity the Holy of Holies had remained empty of everything *except the most gracious presence of God.* But that, too, was lost even *before Jesus was crucified.*

He said, "O Jerusalem! City that murders the prophets and M 23:37 stones the messengers God sends to you! How often have I longed p.90 to gather all your children in my arms, as a hen gathers her brood L 13:34 under her wings! But you would not let me. And now – look! There is your Temple, forsaken by God. And I tell you that, from now on, you will never see me again until the time when you say, "Blessed is he who comes in the name of the Lord!"

And, as he approached the city as King, riding in majesty to the cheers of the people, and the waving palms, he wept over it.
L 19:41 He said, "If only you knew, even on this great day, the way that p.84 leads to peace! But no: you cannot see it . . . for a time is coming

when your enemies will lay siege against you. You will be encircled and hemmed in at every point; and they will utterly destroy you and the people within your walls. Not one stone will be left standing on another – because you did not know your God when he came to save you."

Col 1:20

He poured out his love and his healing power for all who came to him; and he willingly gave his own flesh and blood for us, walking steadily through a most terrible death, paying the price of all our sin, that we might be forgiven. 'He only could unlock the gate of heaven and let us in.' And by that one immeasurable and loving sacrifice, he is bringing all things in heaven and earth back to God; that, through his death, he might destroy the devil, who had power over death, and so lead us to heaven.

Heb 2:14

Crowned with glory, Jesus Christ ascended into heaven.

1ST CENTURY AD – in AD 70 Herod's Temple was pounded to rubble by the Romans. It has never been rebuilt.

After his Resurrection, Jesus' apostles and disciples continued to meet to worship God. They worshipped him as a blessed Trinity of Father, Son and Holy Spirit. And Christians all down the ages have done the same.

We have built temples, churches and chapels – some simple, some ornate. At present we are re-learning that it is impossible for the Holy Spirit to be monopolised within the walls of one church building, and that the people outside it – the 'others,' are not necessarily heretics!

The Holy Spirit cannot be confined. We might as well try to catch the waters of Niagara in an eggcup! We cannot even contain the love of God within our own hearts – it has to flow through – and out to others to remain true and real.

And we are as nothing – temples, churches, chapels, bishops, pastors, all of us – unless the Holy Spirit is present within us. But when he is present, then:

GOD'S CHURCH LIVES WITHIN THE HEARTS AND MINDS OF HIS PEOPLE

JEWISH RELIGIOUS FEASTS

FEAST – celebration, festival, fete, holiday.

The Festivals of the Israelites were appointed by God –

(i)   to remember great events in their past

(ii) so that the ceremonies and the dignities of divine service would keep them steadfast in their religion

(iii) to give them instruction. At these religious assemblies the Law was read and explained

(iv) to renew acquaintance, correspondence and friendship bonds between the tribes and families; they would all come into the Holy City from the countryside and meet at least three times a year.

The most ancient of the feasts are –

THE SABBATH – to remember the world's creation – the 7th day of the week.

THE SABBATICAL YEAR – every 7th year – entirely set apart for rest.

JUBILEE YEAR – every 49th year.

Nisan
(March)

THE PASSOVER – to remember the Exodus. When the Israelites left Egypt God told them, through Moses, that this date was now to be the beginning of the Jewish year.

Having been forewarned and instructed by God, the children of the Israelites were protected from the terrible action of the destroying angel in the last of the plagues of Egypt. When the angel passed through Egypt at midnight, all the first-born of man and beast were struck dead. But the Israelites were protected by the blood of the sacrificial lamb – the Paschal lamb – from the Hebrew: 'pasach' = to leap, pass over. See Exodus 11 and 12; also Cruden p. 247 about Hyssop.

G
(sin)

Jesus was killed at Passover time. The blood of the Lamb was shed to save us all from sin and death.

The bread-kneading bowls had all been packed for the journey – wrapped in the mantles worn by the Israelites. Unleavened bread was eaten. The Feast of:

UNLEAVENED BREAD – runs concurrently with the Feast of the Passover. See Ex 12:14-20 and Ex 13:3-10; also Matt 26:17 and Luke 22:1.

Sivan
(May)

PENTECOST – fifty days after Passover. Sometimes called the Feast of Weeks because it comes seven weeks after Passover. It is a one-day celebration when the Israelites give thanks for being able to enjoy the fruits of their labours.

Also on the Day of Pentecost God delivered the Law from Mount Sinai – in the 11th century BC – and the Holy Spirit came to the disciples in Jerusalem in the 1st century AD.

Tisri
(Sept)
see also
p. (viii)

TABERNACLES OR TENTS – the Tabernacle was the sacred tent, or pavilion, constructed by the Hebrews under the precise instructions which Moses received from God. It housed the Ark of the Covenant. In the Tabernacle the Jews offered sacrifices to God, and performed their most sacred rituals. It was transported from place to place during the Israelites' nomadic years until King Solomon built the first Temple in 960 BC.

Celebrated after the September harvest, this eight-day Feast of Tabernacles was so-called because it was kept under green tents or arbours, to remember their tent-dwelling days and that they were, after all, but pilgrims in this world. It was one of the three most

solemn feasts at which all males had to present themselves before
Ex 23:16-17 the Lord. They also gave thanks that the harvest was safely gathered in.

Caslev
(Nov-Dec)
see also
p. (vi)
THE FEAST OF DEDICATION OR THE FEAST OF LIGHTS — this was to remember the re-dedication of the Temple by Judas Maccabeus in 165 BC after its desecration by Antiochus Epiphanes.

After they had defeated Gorgia's army, Judas Maccabeus, and his brethren found the Temple forsaken and profaned — the courts full of thick brambles, the doors burnt, the altar desecrated and the buildings in ruins. They wept when they saw it. Then they set to work cleaning everything, employing the priests in demolishing the profaned altar, and they built a new altar of rough stone. They re-fitted the Most Holy Place and the Sanctuary (the Holy Place), replacing the sacred table for the shewbread, the golden candlestick and the altar of perfumes. They reverently lit the lamps, put the loaves on the golden table and set light to the incense. They offered sacrifices and burnt offerings and performed the re-dedication of the Temple with all possible solemnity — in eight days.

For more information, see Maccabeus II in the Apocrypha — Chap 10 and 'Jesus and His Times.'

*(A Complete Concordance of the Old and New Testament –
Alexander Cruden)*

THE LINE OF DESCENT
FROM ADAM TO JOSEPH

Matt.
1:1-17
Luke 3:
23-38

ADAM	ABRAHAM	Ozias (Uzziah)
Seth	Isaac	Joatham
Enosh	Jacob	Achaz (Ahaz)
Cainan	Judas	Hezekiah (700 BC)
Mahalalel	Phares	Manasseh
Jared	(md Zara of Thamar)	Amon
Enoch	Esrom	Josiah (650 BC)
Methuselah	Aram	Jechoniah
(about 2,000 BC)	Aminadab	(Jehoiachin)
Lamech	Naasson	Shealtiel
NOAH	Salmon	(born in Babylon
Shem	Boaz of Rachab	Zerubbabel
Arpachshad	(md Ruth	Abiud
Cainan	Obe	Eliakim
Shelag	Jesse	Azor
Eber	DAVID (1,000 BC)	Sadoc
Peleg	SOLOMON (900 BC)	Aehim
Reu	Rchoboam	Eliud
Serug	Abijah	Eleazar
Nahor	Asa	Matthan
Terah	Jehosophat	Jacob
	Joram	JOSEPH (md MARY)

Matt 1:1   "The book of the generation of Jesus Christ, the Son of David, the Son of Abraham."

Matt 1:17   "There were thus fourteen generations in all from Abraham to David, fourteen from David until the deportation to Babylon, and fourteen from the deportation until the Messiah."

Luke 3:23   "When Jesus began his work he was about thirty years old. He was the son, so people thought, of Joseph . . ." Luke traces the descent through David's son, Nathan – partially different from Matthew's version of the descent through Solomon (see page 12). Luke's version avoids the curse of Jechoniah (Jehoiachin) (Jer. 36:30).

Matt 1:18   "This was the way that Jesus Christ was born: his mother, Mary, was betrothed to Joseph, but before they were married she found that she had conceived by the Holy Spirit . . . « A virgin shall conceive, and bear a Son, and he will be called Emmanuel – God is

Isa. 7:14   with us. »"

Matt 22:41   "When the Pharisees gathered together, Jesus asked them, "What do you think about the Messiah? Whose descendant is he?" "He is David's descendant," they replied. "Why then," Jesus asked, "did the Spirit inspire David to refer to him as 'Lord'? For David said, 'The Lord said to my Lord, « Sit here at my right side until I make your enemies your footstool.»' If David called him 'Lord', how can the Messiah be David's descendant?" No one was able to answer Jesus a single word.

(By God's design, His Son was born of the Virgin Mary, into the House of David by her marriage to Joseph. Joseph, following God's direction through the archangel Gabriel, gave to Mary, and the baby Jesus, not only his loving care and protection, but also his name. His marriage, according to Jewish Law, would surely have put the baby Jesus firmly into the House of David).

THE ANCIENT PROPHECIES

Malachi 3:1
Isaiah 40:3 "« Behold! I will send my messenger . . . the voice of him that crieth in the wilderness, 'Prepare ye the way of the Lord! Make straight in the desert a highway for our God!' . . . and he shall prepare the way before me; and the Lord whom you seek shall suddenly come to his Temple »"

Malachi 4:2 "« Unto you who honour my name shall the Sun of Righteousness arise with healing in his wings »"

Malachi 4:5
M 17:10-13
Mk 9:11-13 "« Behold, I will send Elijah, the prophet, before the coming of the dreadful Day of the Lord. He will go before him as a forerunner, possessed by the Spirit, and the power of Elijah, to reconcile father and child, to convert the rebellious to the ways of the righteous, to prepare a people that shall be fit for the Lord »"

Isaiah 7:14 "Therefore the Lord himself shall give you a sign: « Behold, a virgin shall conceive and bear a Son, and shall call his name 'Emmanuel' – God is with us »"

Micah 5:2 "« But thou, Bethlehem Ephrata, though thou be little among the thousands of Judah, yet out of thee shall he come forth unto me that is to be ruler in Israel, whose goings forth have been from of old, from everlasting »"

Isaiah 9:6 "For unto us a child is born; unto us a son is given. And the government shall be upon his shoulders.* And his name shall be called – Wonderful, Counsellor, the mighty God; the everlasting Father, the Prince of Peace. Of the increase of his government and peace there shall be no end – upon the throne of David, and upon his kingdom – to order it and to establish it with judgment and with justice from henceforth even for ever . . . The zeal of the Lord of Hosts shall accomplish it."

*("The Royal dignity he wears" – Moffatt)

Isa.53:6 "All we like sheep have gone astray; we have turned, every one, to his own way; and the Lord hath laid on him the iniquity of us all."

Malachi 3:2 " . . . but who may abide the day of his coming? And who shall stand when he appeareth? For he is like a refiner's fire. . . »"